BRITAIN'S INLAND WATERW...

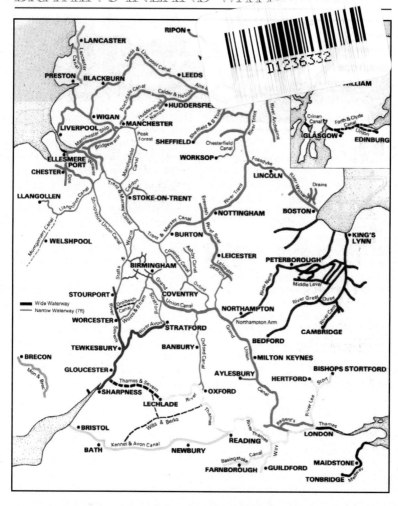

Published by Waterways World Ltd,
The Well House, High Street, Burton-on-Trent, Staffordshire DE14 1JQ, England
Researched and Edited by Euan Corrie
Maps and Artwork by Branch Out Design, Bretby, Burton-on-Trent

First Edition 2002

One of a series of guides covering the Inland Waterways of England and Wales

British Library Cataloguing in Publication Data
A Catalogue Record for this book is available from the British Library
ISBN 1 870002 11 3
Printed in England by Information Press, Eynsham

Introduction

This guide covers the entire 87 miles of the Kennet & Avon Navigation from its junction with the river Thames at Reading to Hanham Lock, near Bristol on the river Avon. Also covered is the semi-tidal section of the Avon (beyond Hanham Lock), the Feeder Canal and Bristol's Floating Harbour. The guide, which starts at the Reading end, follows the westward course of the canal along the river Kennet section from Reading to Newbury, then on to the canal section from Newbury to Bath, and finally on to the river Avon from Bath to Bristol.

It contains information about navigating the waterway, facilities for boating and shopping, and places of interest within walking distance of the canal. Moreover, towpath walkers and those who enjoy exploring canals by car are also catered for. So, whatever your interests are, we hope that you will find this guide useful. Have a good trip and enjoy discovering the Kennet & Avon Canal.

Acknowledgements

The editor is grateful to a great may people who have assisted in the production of this guide. In particular David Harris undertook much of the initial research, Philippa Corrie acted as boat captain, car navigator, clerk and secretary on subsequent trips. Thanks are also due to the staff of British Waterways and members and staff of the Kennet & Avon Canal Trust for invaluable assistance in checking many details. The Aylesbury Canal Society's Launderette List is, as always, an invaluable aid.

The Kennet & Avon Navigation — A Brief History

The waterway covered by this guide actually comprises three separate navigations; the river Kennet from the Thames at Reading to Newbury; the river Avon from Hanham to Bath; and the Kennet & Avon Canal which connected the two rivers.

The river Kennet was the first to be made navigable and was opened in 1723. Four years later navigation works to the river Avon were completed to enable craft to reach Bath.

Although a meeting of interested parties had been held at Marlborough in 1788, it was not until 1794 that they succeeded in obtaining an Act authorising work to commence on a canal to link the two rivers. By 1799 the canal was open from Reading to Great Bedwyn, but delays in constructing the great flight of locks at Devizes prevented completion until 1810.

A successful period followed, but the building of the Great Western Railway in 1841 signalled the start of a decline and ten years later the canal was acquired by the railway company. Traffic was discouraged, maintenance standards deteriorated, and by 1910 through commercial carrying had ceased completely.

The canal remained open, although navigable only with difficulty, until 1951, when the newly formed British Transport Commission, which had acquired the canal when the railways were nationalised, closed it.

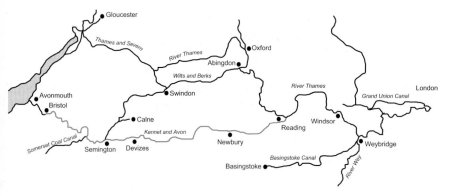

The Kennet & Avon Canal and connections to the waterways of Southern England

The Kennet & Avon Canal Trust (K&ACT) was formed in 1962 (as successor to the Kennet & Avon Canal Association) with the aim of restoring the canal to full navigation and as a public amenity. The work of the Trust has been to plan the restoration programme in partnership with British Waterways and to co-ordinate the support of Local Authorities and Government Agencies. In the early years, the Trust organised working parties and money raising events, later concentrating wholly on raising the huge sums needed to fund complete lock rebuilding and canal-bed re-lining. In the 28 years leading up to the Royal re-opening ceremony in August 1990, the Trust raised £2.8m towards restoration costs. Although the canal was open there remained a whole host of further problems to face. One of these was solving the inherent water supply problems and improving services and facilities for boaters and the public. The Trust took this on and with British Waterways and the local authorities succeeded in providing a £1m back pumping system which returns used lockage water to the top of Devizes Locks. The total cost of full repairs and works to achieve a sustainable future for the whole waterway was assessed at £29m. This was the background to a bid to the Heritage Lottery Fund in 1995. In 1996 a grant of £25m was awarded and work started in 1997. This grant was the largest ever given by the Heritage Lottery Fund to a single project.

The canal's re-opening has not only re-established the inland waterway link between London and Bristol (utilising the Thames from London to Reading) but has also re-connected the waterway to the main canal network.

Navigating the Kennet & Avon Canal

Licences

Addresses of all the authorities and organisations which can provide further information are listed on page 12

River Thames

Boat owners and hirers planning to enter the Kennet & Avon from the main canal network i.e. from the Oxford Canal at Oxford or from the Grand Union Canal at Brentford, will require a licence for passage through the Thames. Registration forms and details of charges may be obtained from the Environment Agency at Reading (see page 12). Transit Licences are also issued by the lock keepers at Osney (for craft joining the river via the Dukes Cut or via Isis Lock at

Oxford), at Teddington Lock (for boats joining the river from the tideway and Blakes Lock for those entering from the Kennet & Avon Canal). The Environment Agency and British Waterways (see below) jointly offer a 'Gold Licence' for craft regularly using both authorities' waterways.

Kennet & Avon Canal

All craft, whether powered or unpowered, including canoes and dinghies, must have a British Waterways Pleasure Boat Licence when navigating the Kennet & Avon between Reading and Hanham Lock. Details of licensing are obtainable from the local British Waterways Waterway Manager at Devizes (01380 722859) or British Waterways' Watford headquarters.

River Avon

If you wish only to cruise the river Avon between Hanham and Bath, you will need a British Waterways' River Registration Certificate, available from British Waterways (above).

Bristol City Docks

British Waterways' jurisdiction on the Avon ends at Hanham Lock (No 1) which is also the tidal limit of the river. West of Hanham, the navigation authority is Bristol City Council which is also responsible for the city's Feeder Canal, Floating Harbour and Docks. For craft visiting Bristol, short-term licences (for 24 hours, 48 hours, 7 days, or per 15 days to a maximum of 30 days) are available from the Harbour Master's Office. These licences are also available from Netham Lock, Bristol Marina and Cumberland Basin Entrance Lock. It is essential to have an anchor for the tidal and river sections. A booklet entitled *Bristol Harbour, Information for Boat Owners*, published by the Bristol City Docks, is essential reading and can be obtained from the Harbour Master's Office or from the Netham Lock keeper.

Navigation Notes

River Kennet

Rising in the chalk hills above Marlborough, the Kennet is not only the main source of supply to the canal east of Kintbury but forms much of the navigation channel as it makes its way towards Kennet Mouth at Reading where it joins the Thames. Whilst there are no water supply problems on this section, heavy rainfall can cause the river level to rise rapidly and create fast currents. You should take particular care to compensate for strong side currents when entering locks and lock cuttings.

On both rivers always moor with your bows pointing up-stream and allow sufficient slack on mooring lines to compensate for changes in level. The current is always faster through bridge arches and between bridge piers so do not attempt to turn up-stream of bridges.

Devizes Flight

The Devizes Flight (locks 22–50) is open daily for the boats to begin their passage between 8am and 2pm (1pm in winter). Passages are under BW lock keepers' supervision. Lock 50 (Devizes Top Lock) is locked between 4.30pm and 8am daily.

For those navigating the Devizes Flight a 'Certificate of Completion' is available from British Waterways, Devizes office, price £5.

River Avon

This is a wide and deep river with lock cuttings and unprotected weirs. Care should be taken during and after heavy rainfall when the river flow and levels can increase considerably. The river is tidal up to Hanham, however, high spring tides can reach up to Keynsham Lock. When the river Avon is in spate the Bath lock flight will be locked.

Between Hanham and Netham the river is affected by ordinary Spring tides which flow over Netham weir on several days each month. On 'stopgate' tides the lock at Netham has to be worked normally as opposed to the usual situation of having all its gates secured open. On these occasions it is simpler to wait for river levels to return to normal when the reduced current and open gates at Netham make navigation altogether simpler. The lock keepers at Hanham or Netham will be pleased to recommend suitable passage times in advance or a tide table can be obtained from the Harbour Master (above). For information about entering The Feeder Canal and Bristol's Floating Harbour, see under Bristol City Docks on page 4

Navigating from Sharpness to Bristol

The Waterway and Dock Authorities at Bristol and Sharpness do not recommend this passage for inland craft. However, owners of suitable private craft intending to navigate from the Gloucester & Sharpness Canal to Bristol via the tidal Severn and Avon (or vice-versa) should seek information about tide times, pilots, charts, safety equipment and navigational aids either from the Harbour Master at Bristol Docks (see under Bristol City Docks) or from British Waterways at Sharpness, (01453 811644). It should be noted that, subject to weather conditions, a convoy of inland craft makes the passage from Sharpness to Bristol annually in August to attend the Bristol Regatta –details can be obtained from Leisure Services, Bristol City Council, (0117 922-3521). (Note: The distance from Bristol to Sharpness via Avonmouth and the river Severn is 30 miles; the passage time is 10 hours, four of which are spent anchored or aground waiting for the tide. The tidal range, which is in excess of 14 metres, is the second largest in the world).

Stoppages

From time to time, particularly in the winter months (Nov-March), it may become necessary for BW to carry out maintenance work on the waterway. Alternatively, a dry spring or summer may result in restrictions due to shortage of water. Either of these circumstances may result in sections being closed or 'stopped'. For details of stoppages telephone: Canalphone South (01923 201402). To obtain assistance or report emergencies outside office hours dial 0800 4799947 for Freephone Canals. Have details of the waterway and the nearest lock or bridge number or similar landmark ready.

Speed

There is usually a speed limit of 4mph on the canal and 6mph on rivers. Even this low speed is often too fast. Remember – an excessive wash or breaking wave causes bank erosion and damage to moored craft as well as being a general nuisance. Slow down when approaching or passing moored craft, other craft under way, locks, bridges, tunnels, engineering works and on bends. When the view ahead is obstructed, slow down, sound your horn and listen.

Rule of the Road

Craft meeting should steer to the right and pass each other left to left. If you do not intend to do this you must make it clear to the oncoming boat. When a vessel is being towed from the bank pass outside the vessel to avoid fouling the towing line - never pass between the towed vessel and the bank. Craft travelling with the current on rivers or tideway have the right of way over those heading against the flow.

Depth

If you could see the canal drained of its water you'd be surprised how shallow it is, especially at the edges, the cross section being a shallow 'V' rather than 'U' shaped. Keep to the centre of the channel except when passing oncoming boats. This is particularly important on sections which have been concreted (see text accompanying maps for location). Give way to larger craft which require deeper water. You may find yourself aground if you have moved out of the centre channel to pass another boat. This is nothing to worry about. You should be able to reverse off, but if that doesn't work, push yourself off with your boat pole.

Mooring

Always, unless specifically indicated to the contrary, moor against the towpath side of the canal. Steer your boat in bow first, put the engine into neutral and then pull the stern of your boat in with your rope. Keeping the propeller turning near to the bank could seriously damage the propeller and both the bed and bank of the canal. When pushing off again, ensure that the boat is well away from the bank before engaging forward gear.
• Do not moor too near bridges or locks so as to obstruct full size craft cruising the canal.
• Do not moor on bends or in winding holes.
• Do not moor in the short pounds of a flight of locks.
• Do not stretch ropes across towpaths where they will obstruct and endanger towpath users.

Safety First

Remember always that prevention is better than cure. Wear non-slip footwear and beware of slippery lock sides and gates in wet weather. Beware of low bridges – some of which are lower in the middle (sometimes with supporting girders) than at each end. Make sure that your crew is aware of the presence of a low bridge - especially those sitting on the cabin top. Before you enter a long tunnel, tell the crew to switch on the cabin lights (the cabin lights shining on the walls are useful to the helmsman). Ensure that torches are handy when entering tunnels and for use at night.
It is advisable to be able to swim when contemplating a holiday afloat. Non-swimmers and young children should wear life jackets. When walking along the side-decks use the handrails on the cabin top.

Make sure that you know the position and method of operation of the fire extinguishers provided on the boat. Take a basic first aid kit with you including insect repellent. It is a good rule to spend the first night aboard making sure that you know where everything is, how emergency equipment works and reading the instructions or handbooks on essential equipment provided by the owner.

Tunnels

Canal craft should be equipped with a suitable headlamp for navigating tunnels which should be trained slightly to the right to avoid dazzling oncoming steerers in wide tunnels. Torches should also be carried. Go dead slow when approaching other craft but do not stop in tunnels except in an emergency.
There is only one tunnel on the Kennet & Anon Canal, Bruce Tunnel (sometimes called Savernake Tunnel) 502yds long, which has no towpath. Unpowered craft are prohibited from passing through the tunnel. Bear in mind that this navigation is used by wide beam vessels which cannot pass others in the tunnel.

Bridges

With the exception of two swing bridges in Bristol's Floating Harbour, none of the many hand and power-operated bridges on the Kennet & Avon are manned. This calls for attention to Bridge Operating Instructions – read them carefully before carrying them out and make sure that your crew fully understands what has to be done, particularly where road traffic controls are involved. Having said that, the K&A offers the boater a variety of swing bridges and one of the most sophisticated lift bridges on the canal system (at Aldermaston). Some are power operated and require a standard British Waterways Sanitary Station key to gain access to the controls. This key is also required for securing devices at many more. Others require a standard British Waterways windlass for jacking-up, unlocking holding chains or for operating road barriers.

Note: Do not stand on the roof of the boat or anywhere along the gunwale nearest the bridge deck when passing under lift bridges and never attempt to get off the boat on to the bridge deck.

BW Sanitary Station keys (Yale type)

It is essential to have at least one of these on board not only to gain access to Sanitary Stations and water points but also for unlocking swing bridges. Keys are available for sale direct from British Waterways (see under Useful Addresses) and from most boat yards and marinas.

Mileage

Reading to Hanham Lock – 87 miles
Hanham to Bristol Docks – 6 miles

Locks

Lock dimensions. In canal parlance, the Kennet & Avon is known as a wide or broad canal, meaning that the waterway, and more particularly the locks, are capable of taking craft of a wide beam (originally up to 14ft). Today, the lock dimensions are:

Reading to Newbury

Length - up to 70ft (21.34m)
Beam – up to 14ft (3.94m)
Headroom 7ft 9in (2.36m)
Draught – up to 3ft (0.91m)

Newbury to Bath

Length – up to 70ft (21.34m)
Beam – up to 12ft 11in (3.94m)
Headroom – 7ft (2.13m)
Draught – up to 3ft (0.91m)

Bath to Hanham Lock

Length – up to 75ft (22.86m)
Beam – up to 16ft (4.88m)
Headroom – 8ft 9in (2.66m)
Draught – up to 3ft (0.91m)

Number of locks – Reading to Hanham – 104 locks.

Note: although the maximum length of locks on the canal section is 70ft, full length narrow beam craft can use these locks by positioning the boat diagonally in the lock.

Where locks are deep and fitted with gate paddles, care should be taken not to raise the paddles too quickly, for if you do, there is a danger of water cascading into the lock and swamping your foredeck; this precaution applies particularly to full length craft. In addition, skippers of full length craft should also beware of catwalks positioned on the inside of some bottom gates. The danger here is that as you ascend, your tiller can catch under the catwalks with disastrous results. It is also advisable to rope both ends of your boat, particularly when ascending, to prevent bobbing about and banging against other craft in the lock.

The original locks of the river Kennet Navigation were turf sided. Their chambers were basically holes in the ground with grass growing on their sloping sides. Owing to rebuilding since the Great Western Railway obtained control of the navigation many of these locks have been reduced from their original Newbury barge dimensions and all have vertical sides below water level. Only that at Garston remains truly turf sided. Take care to keep your boat alongside, and not catching under, the frame of old Broad Gauge rail which is intended to prevent craft settling on the sloping banks.

Monkey Marsh Lock was rebuilt after archeological excavation and recording of the various previous chambers on the site. Unfortunately the result more nearly resembles the catwalks at an oil refinery dock than a reproduction turf sided lock chamber but the same care is needed in locking through. Several of the other chambers have been rebuilt with scalloped brick walls which show the original positions of the vertical members of the frames in the turf sided locks.

Lock Operation

The golden rule is never waste water. The lock drill described below should be followed systematically.

The basic principle of lock operation is that water never passes straight through a lock. It comes in from the top and stays in, or goes out through the bottom without any following it from the top. If you liken the lock itself to a kitchen sink – the top end to the tap and the bottom to the plug – don't turn the tap on until the plug is in, and don't pull the plug out until the tap is off.

Lock-keepers: On the river Thames lock keepers are usually on hand to direct traffic and operate the lock. This is the exception; lock operation on canals and the Bristol Avon is usually undertaken by the boat crew. At busy spots, such as the Caen Hill flight at Devizes lock-keepers may be available to assist and regulate traffic. They may ask you to share a lock with another boat or wait whilst another boat comes through the other way. Obey their instructions but do not necessarily expect that they will do the work for you – that's part of the fun of your holiday.

Staircase Locks: Await you in other parts of the country but will not be encountered on the Kennet & Avon.

How to Operate Locks

A windlass is usually required to fit the paddle spindles of manually operated locks. These will usually be provided on the boat and have two holes of different sizes to take the spindle's squared end. Take care to use the correct sized hole on the spindle as a bad fit is dangerous since the windlass may fly off. In direct contravention of the recommendation of its own paddle gearing committee BW has fitted a mixture of sizes of spindles at numerous locks so constant attention is needed. Do not leave the windlass on the spindle when not winding the paddle up or down – make sure the pawl is in place to stop the paddle falling and remove the windlass so that it cannot fly round if the catch slips.

Those of the crew who operate the paddles must remember that the noise of the engine and rushing water will prevent people on the boat hearing their instructions or them hearing shouts of panic. Those ashore are responsible for keeping an eye on the boat all the time that the lock is filling or emptying to see that it continues to rise or fall steadily. If there is any doubt shut all the paddles quickly and then stop to think and check if the

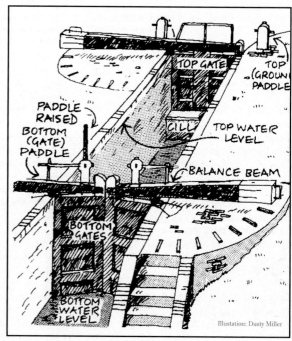

Illustation: Dusty Miller

boat or its ropes and fenders are catching on any part of the lock or other boats. Particularly check that the stem fender does not catch under the top gate or its handrails when going up hill. Boats sharing locks, which is a good way to save water, must lie beside or ahead and astern of one another, never twisted across each other at bow or stern. Like that they will jam as the level alters.

Illustation: Dusty Miller

(1) Going Uphill – Lock Empty
Check that top gates are shut and paddles closed.

Enter the lock and drive the boat to the far end where there will be less turbulence as the lock fills.

Close the bottom gates. See that the bottom gate paddles are closed.

Open top ground paddles (where applicable). Water from these will pass under the boat to the other end of the chamber and hold the boat steadily against the top gate or cill.

Ropes are not usually required to hold a boat steady in narrow locks but will often be a good idea in bigger chambers. A spring running slightly astern from the fore end may be best with some tension being maintained by keeping the engine running in forward gear. Do not tie knots in any rope used in locks, they will jam when it is necessary to adjust the length of line as the water rises or falls and leave the boat hanging in mid air or sunk. Do not try to hold a rope as the lock fills either; take a couple of turns round a cleat or bollard and the extra friction thus gained will help prevent the boat dragging the rope through your hand causing nasty burns as it does so.

In most wide beam locks, such as those on the K&A, where two or more narrowboats could fit alongside one another, a less turbulent ascent for a single boat will result from drawing the top ground paddle on the same side as the boat first. The water will usually pass beneath the boat and help to hold it steadily against the wall.

Open the top gate paddles when their outlets in the gates are submerged (where applicable). Some river Kennet locks have only gate paddles and greater care is needed here to avoid flooding the fore end when going up hill by opening these too much too rapidly.

When the lock is full open the top gates.

Leave the lock. Close the top gates and all paddles.

(2) Going Uphill – Lock Full
Check that there is no boat approaching from above the lock which could save water by descending as you empty the lock for your boat to enter.

If not, close the top gates. See that the top gate and ground paddles are closed.

Open the bottom paddles.

When the lock is empty open the bottom gates and close the bottom gate paddles. Proceed as (1) above.

(3) Going Downhill – Lock Full

A wide beam cruiser leaves Blake's Lock, which is managed by the Environment Agency, for the Kennet & Avon Navigation, controlled by Britsh Waterways.

Picture: Peter Ivernee

Enter the lock and drive the boat to the far end where it will be well clear of the cill near the top gates as the water drops.

Close the top gates. See that the top gate paddles and ground paddles are closed.

Open the bottom gate paddles.

When lock is empty open the bottom gates.

Leave the lock. Close all bottom paddles and gates.

(4) Going downhill – Lock Empty

Check that there is no boat approaching from below the lock which could save water by ascending as you fill the lock for your boat to enter.

Close the bottom gates. See that the bottom gate paddles are closed.

Open the ground paddles.

Open the top gate paddles when submerged (where applicable).

When the lock is full, open the top gates. Proceed as (3) above.

Before leaving a lock see that all paddles are fully and securely closed. On canals it is important to shut the exit gates as well; failure to do so may result in serious flooding of property, stranding of craft through loss of water from the pound above, and possible flooding of craft when the pound is refilled.

It is easiest to pick up lock crew at the lock mouth which saves approaching the shallow canal margins where you may run aground. But in all situations where crew are joining or leaving even a slowly moving boat make them get on or off at the stern. Should they slip they will then get wet after the boat has passed and not fall in where it will pass over them or crush them against a wall. At the stern the steerer is also at hand to put the engine out of gear quickly and assist.

Lift and Swing Bridges

Lift bridges are common on some canals such as the Llangollen or Oxford whilst others, like the K&A, specialise in the swinging variety. Although visually often attractive, these, like low brick arches, have their own special hazards for navigators. If you line your boat up with the coping on the towpath side of the bridge, the roof of your boat should miss the bridge decking, but if the wind catches the boat, or the boat hits the coping and bounces off, you could hit your cabin. When approaching these bridges, never allow anyone to stand at the bows of the boat near to where the cabin might hit the bridge – several tons of boat travelling at up to 4mph could easily crush them between boat and bridge. Never attempt to get off the boat onto the deck of a moveable bridge, this has proved fatal several times.

Use common sense when lifting or swinging the bridges and do not open the bridge if a vehicle is approaching. Where no gate is provided, a member of your crew should warn road traffic.

There are now numerous methods of operating moving bridges. You may be able to let a younger crew member operate the remoter bridges. Elsewhere adult assistance may be important when operating interlocked powered barriers, road traffic lights and sirens before a heavy main road bridge swings clear for the boat to pass. (If nothing happens read the instructions again as there may be a time lock to stop you devastating the rush hour traffic system by opening the bridge during that period.) The electrically powered versions usually require a BW sanitary station key, which will be provided with the boat, others require your lock windlass to operate hydraulic pumps.

Beyond the Towpath

This publication is intended primarily as a guide to the canal but it also includes information on some of the places of interest near the canal. More detailed information can be obtained from local tourist offices. (See the text accompanying the maps for details of Tourist Offices).

Walking the Kennet & Avon Canal

Though canal towpaths are not usually Public Rights of Way, virtually all of that on the K&A is now classified as such. It is no longer an offence for the public to make use of these excellent long-distance footpaths. Some very good canalside walks may be enjoyed by combining lengths of towpaths with the official footpaths and bridleways marked on the appropriate OS Landranger 1:50,000 maps covering the area. Many of these tracks and byways are also marked on the maps in this guide.

Though 'lock-wheeling' is as much part of today's boating as it was in the days of working boats, it is an offence to cycle along the towpath without a permit. These are obtainable from British Waterways local Waterway Manager's office or from BW's Head Office, the Kennet & Avon Canal Trust's shops and their office at Devizes. There are some lengths of towpath where cycling is not permitted, details of which will be sent to applicants along with their free permit which must be displayed on handlebars at all times. Cyclists without a permit are liable to a fine.

Bibliography

Kennet & Avon Canal – A user's Guide to the Waterways between Reading and Bristol by Niall Allsop (Millstream Books).
The Kennet & Avon Canal by Kenneth R. Clew (David & Charles).
The Kennet & Avon Canal – A Journey from Newbury to Bath in 1964 by John Russell (Millstream Books).
Pubs on the Kennet & Avon Canal by Niall Allsop (Millstream Books).
Canals of South-West England by Charles Hadfield (David & Charles)
Through the K&A in 1928 by Motor Boat by J. D. Smith.
Images of the Kennet & Avon by Niall Allsop.

The Wilts & Berks Canal by Jack Dalby.
Somerset Coal Canal Rediscovered by Niall Allsop.
Boating The Kennet & Avon, guide by BW.
Crofton Pumping Station by K&ACT.
Crofton in the Twenties by K&ACT.
Towpath Accommodation Guide by BW.
Claverton Pumping Station by K&ACT.
Monkey Marsh Lock – Detailed account of restoration by K&ACT.
Kennet & Avon Pictorial Guide by K&ACT.

Videos:
Sentimental Journey – a leisurely cruise east to west in 1990, narrated by Johnny Morris.
Ribbon Across England – a personal look at the many attractions of the canal from *Bristol to Reading* by Tim Wheeldon.
The Kennet & Avon Part 1: Reading to Bruce Tunnel and Part 2: Bruce Tunnel to Bristol both by Video Active.
Many of these publications and videos are available from the Kennet & Avon Canal Trust's Canal Centre at Devizes.

Maps and Charts.

GEOprojects map of the Kennet & Avon Canal – fold-out boater's map.
Ordnance Survey maps (Landranger Series) 1:50,000 scale: sheets 175 Reading, 174 Newbury, 173 Swindon, 172 Bristol.
Admiralty Charts: 1165 Avonmouth to Sharpness, 1859 River Avon.
Note: British Waterways publish a range of information leaflets – copies of these may be obtained (free) from BW's Devizes office and Padworth Visitor Centre – see under Useful Addresses.

Useful Addresses
The Environment Agency
Thames Region, Kings Meadow House, Kings Meadow Road, Reading RG1 8DQ (0118 9535000, www.environment-agency.gov.uk). Recorded navigation information 0118 9535620.

A narrowboat enters Sheffield Lock, one of the former turf sided locks on the Kennet which has been restored with distinctive scalloped walls.

Bristol City Docks
Harbour Masters Office, Underfall Yard, Cumberland Road, Bristol BS1 6XG. (0117 903 1484, VHF channel 73 "Bristol Floating Harbour").

British Waterways
Waterway Manager: British Waterways, The Locks, Bath Road, Devizes, Wiltshire SN10 1HB (01380 722859) Fax (01380 729076).
Head Office: British Waterways, Willow Grange, Church Road, Watford, Hertfordshire WD17 4QA (01923 226422). Freephone Canals (for emergencies and out of hours assistance) 0800 47 999 47.
Canalphone South for recorded details of unscheduled stoppages 01923 201402.

Kennet & Avon Canal Trust
Devizes Wharf, Couch Lane, Devizes,

Wiltshire SN10 1EB or at www.katrust.demon.co.uk (01380 721279, Fax 01380 727870, email: administrator@kact.org.uk).
Kennet & Avon Visitor Centre, Canal Cottage, Wharfside, Padworth, Reading, Berks RG7 4JS (0118 9712868).

The Association of Canal Enterprises PO Box 21, Hungerford, Berkshire RG17 9YY (01672 515498, www.k&adirectory.co.uk).

Hire Boat Companies based on the Kennet & Avon Canal

Anglo Welsh Waterway Holidays, Avon Quay, Cumberland Basin, Bristol BS1 6XL (0117 924 1200).

Berry Brook Boats, operate from Burghfield Island but may be contacted at 195 Henley Road, Caversham, Reading RG2 9XD (07831 574673, www.berrybrookboats.co.uk).

Bridge Boats Ltd, are based on the Thames close to Kennetmouth at Frys Island, Reading, Berks RG1 8LD (0118 9590346).

Reading Marine Company, Aldermaston Wharf, Padworth, Reading, RG7 4JS (0118 971 3666, www.readingmarine.com).

The Bruce Trust, PO Box 21, Hungerford, Berkshire RG17 9YY (01672 515498 www.brucetrust.org.uk) operates wide beam craft specially designed to permit disabled and less mobile people to enjoy normal self-drive canal boat holidays from Great Bedwyn and Foxhangers wharves.

Foxhanger Canal Holidays, Foxhanger Wharf, Devizes, Wiltshire SN10 1SS (01380 828795, www.foxhangers.co.uk).

Kennet Cruises, 14, Beech Lane, Earley, Reading, Berks RG5 2PT (0118 9871115).

Sally Boats Ltd, Bradford-on-Avon Marina, Trowbridge Road, Bradford-on-Avon, Wilts BA15 1UD (01225 864923, www.sallyboats.ltd.uk).

Wessex Narrowboats, Wessex Wharf, The Slipway, Staverton Waterside, Trowbridge, Wilts BA14 84P (01225 769847, www.wessexboats.co.uk)

White Horse Boats, 8, Southgate Close, Pans Lane, Devizes, Wilts SN10 5AQ (01380 728504).

Hotel Boats based on the Kennet & Avon Canal
Operate throughout the waterway system, with crew dealing with the navigational hazards and treating their guests to a high degree of comfort and full board accommodation:

Inland Waterway Holiday Cruises, Greenham Lock Cottage, London Road, Newbury, Berkshire RG14 5SN (07831 110811) www.bargeholiday.uk.com

Hotelboat Harlequin operates a wide beam boat between Bristol, London and Lechlade (07703 218239, email: hotelboat@genie.co.uk) www.harlequinhotelboat.co.uk

Public Transport

Buses – National Express (Nationwide service) (08705 80 80 80).

Reading Buses (Local bus service and London service) (0118 959 4000).

West Berkshire Bus Enquiries 0870 608 2608

Wiltshire Bus Line (0845 709 0899, email buses@wiltshire.gov.uk).

First Badgerline (01225 464446, at Bath and 0117 9558211 at Bristol).

Bristol City Line (0117 955 3231)

Train information is best obtained from the National Enquiry Number (08457 484950)

STAVERTON MARINA
HOME OF
Wessex Narrowboats

At Staverton, (Parsons Bridge No 167) on the western side of the Caen Hill flight, we offer full marina and canal boat services for boaters on the glorious K & A Canal.

- ❖ Diesel, Coal, Gas & Pump-out
- ❖ Dayboats for Hire
- ❖ Extensive range of Chandlery
- ❖ DIY Fit-Out Consultancy Service
- ❖ Yanmar Shire & Beta Marine Agents
- ❖ Secure overnight and short-term moorings
- ❖ Narrowboat re-models, refits and makeovers
- ❖ On-board Electrical Services, Inverters/Batteries
- ❖ Full boat building and fit-out services – narrow and broad beam
- ❖ Corgi Gas Registered British Waterways Boat Safety Examiner on-site
- ❖ Boats for sale through our proactive brokerage – We work to sell your boat 24 hours a day!
- ❖ Emergency dry dock repairs and all types of scheduled maintenance
- ❖ Not forgetting our superlative narrowboat hire fleet

Wessex Narrowboats, Staverton Marina, Trowbridge, Wiltshire BA14 8UP
Tel: 01225 769847 Fax: 01225 769849 e-mail: hire@wessexboats.co.uk
Web: www.wessexboats.co.uk

Reading

All services. No EC. MD Wed, Thurs, Fri and Sat. Banks. Tourist Info Town Hall (0118 9566226), stocks local waterway maps, guides and walk books as well as cards featuring the Kennet. Launderettes: 28, Earley Road (0118 9264906) and 267, Basingstoke Road (0118 9863254).

Reading, which stands on the banks of both the Thames and Kennet rivers first appeared on the map in the 11th Century, when Henry I founded a great Benedictine Abbey alongside the river Kennet. The Abbots, with their Royal patronage dominated life in the town for 400 years controlling navigation, milling and fishing rights as well as regulating trade (mainly wool), industry (cloth making) and the markets; they even hired and fired the mayor.

After the Civil War, during which Reading changed hands several times from King to Parliament and back again and which had a devastating effect on trade, the town entered a 'lack lustre' period until the 18th Century when trade and industry began to flourish again along with improved communications. The Kennet Navigation, opened in 1723 linked the town with Newbury and, in 1810

on completion of the Kennet & Avon Canal, with Bristol thereby opening up an east–west trade route with London via the Thames. The Great Bath Road (A4) passed through the town bringing trade and custom and the coming of the Great Western Railway, in 1840, introduced a modern and fast means of transport.

Four men of vision led Reading's revival – John Simmonds established a Brewery in 1785, which is now part of the Courage Group, while John Sutton began his seed business in 1806. But it was John Huntley and George Palmer who joined forces to produce the famous Huntley & Palmers biscuits which really put Reading back on the map. Through its extensive Kennet wharves, the biscuit company used the waterway to bring flour in and to transport the biscuits out, a waterborne trade which continued until the Second World War. Sadly, biscuits are no longer made in Reading. Oscar Wilde brought notoriety to the town in his Ballad of Reading Goal during his two year imprisonment there. Today, the casual moorer in the town centre ties up by the impenetrable walls of the prison which stands alongside the Abbey ruins in Chestnut Walk.

Meanwhile, Reading today is very much a

Picture: Euan Corrie

A winter view of the Oracle Centre in Reading which clearly illustrates the constricted river Kennet at this point which looks even less navigable than usual in this view taken when rain had raised the river's level.

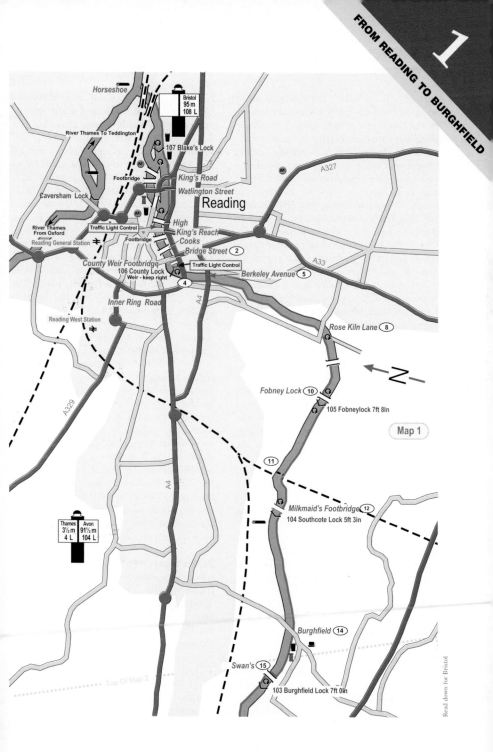

Horseshoe

Bristol
95 m
108 L

River Thames To Teddington

107 Blake's Lock

King's Road

Footbridge

Watlington Street

Reading

Caversham Lock

River Thames
From Oxford

High

Reading General Station

Traffic Light Control

Footbridge

King's Reach

Cooks

Bridge Street (2)

County Weir Footbridge

106 County Lock
Weir - keep right

Traffic Light Control

Berkeley Avenue (5)

(4)

Inner Ring Road

Reading West Station

A329

A4

Rose Kiln Lane (8)

←Z–

Fobney Lock (10)

105 Fobneylock 7ft 8In

Map 1

(11)

Thames | Avon
3½ m | 91½ m
4 L | 104 L

Milkmaid's Footbridge (12)

104 Southcote Lock 5ft 3in

A4

Burghfield (14)

Swan's (15)

Top Of Map 2

103 Burghfield Lock 7ft 0in

Read down for Bristol

part of 'Silicon Valley', the result of major computer and electronic companies moving to the town; in addition, leading insurance companies are concentrated in the town centre headed by the 'Pru'. A new and extensive Shopping Centre coupled with Reading's two main shopping streets – Broad Street and Friar Street – cater for all shopping needs. The oracle centre, completed in 2000 has completely changed the surroundings of the river navigation alongside the Brewery Gut in the process providing several major retail outlets in pedestrianised surroundings. It also houses numerous places of entertainment, bars, cafés and restaurants. Nearby in Southampton Street is the Hop Leaf pub which brews some of the real ale it serves on the premises.

Places of interest Blakes Lock Museum, Gasworks Road, off Kenavon Drive (0118 939 9800) (Tues to Fri 10–5pm in school holidays only and Sat, Sun & Bank Hol Mons 2–5pm all year: Admission free). Fascinating displays featuring Reading's waterways, trades and industries in 19th & 20th centuries. Well worth a visit especially since the museum is under threat of closure at the time of writing early in 2001. Museum of English Rural Life, University of Reading, Whiteknights Park (0118 9318663) (Tues–Sat 10–1, 2–4.30pm all year, featuring agriculture, craft and country life of last 200 years). Reading Abbey and Forbury Gardens, The Forbury (Open all year round) – remains of 12th century Abbey and formal gardens. Reading Museum, Blagrave Street (0118 939 9800, www.readingmuseum.org.uk) (Tue–Sat 10am–4pm, Sun & B.Hols 11–4pm), has a collection of Roman artefacts.

Eating out The town has a good choice of eating places from in-store, hotel and fast-food to Italian, Indian, Chinese and Spanish. In St Mary's Butts are – Pizza Express, (seven days a week from noon to midnight),

Nino's Italian restaurant and Muswell's Continental Wine Bar and Cafe serving snacks and meals. In Castle Street are Los Amogos Tapas Bar & Restaurant and Sweeney & Todd, a highly recommended pub, wine bar and eating house noted for its home-made pies. The 15th century half-timbered George Hotel in King Street has 3 bars and a Berni Inn (7-days). On the opposite side of Chestnut Walk moorings is The Warwick Arms (Morlands) serving lunch Mon-Sat and dinner Mon-Thurs. On Kennet Side above Blakes Lock is Ben's Bar and Thai Restaurant, providing a relaxed wine bar atmosphere. Just below High Bridge is Duke's Restaurant & Wine Bar serving lunches Mon-Fri and dinner Mon–Sat.

Kennet Mouth A more uninspiring (and un-signposted) junction with the Thames to one of Britain's most glorious waterways cannot be imagined with its glut of gasometers and railway bridges – and a derelict building to boot! However, two historic features provide relief in the form of a wooden 'horseshoe' pedestrian bridge (circa 1891) carrying the Thames towpath over the canal entrance. The first of the two railway bridges is a Brunel masterpiece which was built for the Great Western Railway, that opened through to Bristol in 1840, competing with the Kennet & Avon Canal. Both structures are listed and there is a plaque to Brunel's work on the towpath side.

Bridge Boats ▬ ▌ ⚲ ⚓ (0118 9590346, www.bridgeboats.com) are based at Frys Island on the Thames, close to Kennet Mouth, but licence their narrow beam hire craft for use on the Kennet & Avon as well as the Thames. Pump-out. Engine repairs, traditional, boat building and repairs, Slipway.

Thames & Kennet Marina (0118 948 2911) on former gravel pits alongside the Thames opposite Kennet Mouth provides full marina services.

Kennet Side and Blakes Lock The Kennet heads south-west into the centre of Reading past a school, a row of terraced houses and the Jolly Angler (Courage) pub (lack of depth close-in and high railings make it difficult to tie up here). Blakes Lock, formerly a 'flash' lock about half a mile from the junction is the only lock on the navigation not maintained by BW but by the Environment Agency. Immediately behind the towpath side houses is a general store and newsagent. Beyond, on the backwater, is Blakes Lock Museum in a former Victorian Pumphouse. The official public moorings in Reading are at Chestnut Walk which can be reached by navigating up the backwater or by turning right into it from upstream, approximately half a mile above Blakes Lock (an overnight mooring charge is payable). Access to the town centre shops and Blakes Lock Museum is easiest from the Chestnut Walk moorings. On the main river above Blakes Lock is the Fisherman's Cottage (bar meals lunchtime and evenings).

Picture: Peter Ivermee

A pair of working boats seen from the ring road bridge as they leave County Lock in Reading. Note the short length of landing stage available for boats heading down stream and its closeness to the black floating weir boom. The traffic light controlling passage through the constricted Brewery Gut may just be seen on the right bank below the lock.

High Bridge and Brewery Gut Modern office buildings and a landscaped canalside walk have replaced a busy wharf area leading up to High Bridge (circa 1787). However, it is still possible to moor here on the towpath side for access to the shops. On the opposite side is the 'press button' traffic light control for Brewery Gut beyond, a 500-yard narrow channel with blind bends and a potentially hazardous passage when the river is fast flowing. Mooring is prohibited in this restricted section. It is a 'one-way' system, so stop by the light, press the button and wait for green. Crews who do not remain on board will find the riverside walk through the new Oracle Centre up to County Lock a little indirect. The reason is historical in that, at the turn of the century, the local Simmonds Brewery was allowed to develop its site right to the water's edge. This and surrounding property has now been redeveloped as 'Reading Oracle Centre'.

County Lock to Burghfield

County Lock (106) is adjacent to a weir which can cause tricky conditions at times of flood as can the currents into and out of several of the backwaters on this river navigation so beware. Both Fobney and Southcote locks have pumping stations of a by-gone era, the former retaining its Victorian charm and filter beds, now used for breeding fish by the Environment Agency and has been converted into a family home. Burghfield Island, where the river temporarily diverts, has a long-established Boat Club south of the fine stone arch bridge. Just beyond the bridge is The Cunning Man (Bass), a family pub with extensive gardens, children's play area and canal bank moorings. Food is served all week in bars and restaurant and there are pool tables. Opposite the pub is Bridge Cafe serving hot meals (and take-away). Kennet Cruises operate their trip boat *Lancing* from outside the pub.

Kennet Cruises (01734 871115, www.kennetcruises.co.uk). Trip boat, also 4-berth hire boat available for weekly, short break and day hire, facilities for berth holders at Southcote moorings may be available to other craft by appointment.

Berry Brook Boats (07831 574673, www.berrybrookboats.co.uk). Hire craft from Burghfield Island with the additional option of one way trips to Bradford on Avon.

Burghfield Lock to Sulhamstead

Burghfield Lock was the first to be re-built by the Kennet & Avon Canal Trust and is the shortest on the canal. Originally turf sided (like most of the original locks on the Kennet Navigation between Reading and Newbury), it is now steel piled and has the catwalks on the inside of the bottom gates which are a potential hazard for skippers of long craft (see under 'Locks' on page 7).The scenery now assumes a familiar Kennet valley pattern alternating between tree-lined stretches and water meadows, often with grazing cattle. Leading up to the steel structured span of the M4 overbridge are one or two blind bends so don't get too carried away with the scenery! And then there's Garston Lock (see page 22), the only surviving example of a turf-sided lock (its construction is described on page 7). To the south is Theale Lake, one of many flooded gravel pits providing recreational sports of different kinds while beyond is Sheffield Lock (see page 10), the first of three with unusual 'scalloped' brickwork built up on the base of the original toe walls of the turf-sided chambers. Theale Swing Bridge is power operated, needing a BW key to activate the controls. South of the navigation the Fox & Hounds serves Adnams, Badger and Wadworth ales and bar meals lunchtime and evening. Theale village half a mile north of the bridge has a Post Office, baker, bank and a supermarket plus pubs serving food, the Old Lamb Hotel &

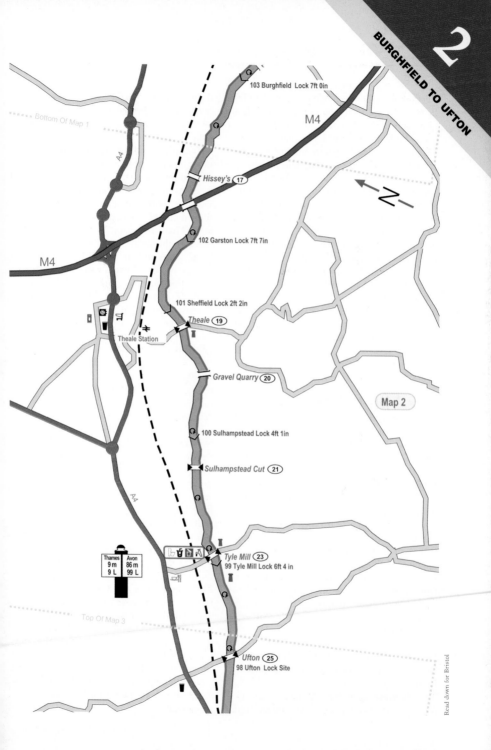

103 Burghfield Lock 7ft 0in

M4

Bottom Of Map 1

Hissey's 17

102 Garston Lock 7ft 7in

M4

101 Sheffield Lock 2ft 2in

Theale 19

Theale Station

Gravel Quarry 20

Map 2

100 Sulhampstead Lock 4ft 1in

Sulhampstead Cut 21

Thames	Avon
9 m	86 m
9 L	99 L

Tyle Mill 23
99 Tyle Mill Lock 6ft 4 in

Top Of Map 3

Ufton 25
98 Ufton Lock Site

Read down for Bristol

Restaurant, a Chinese Restaurant and an off licence. All are in the main street. Theale's unusually large Church – Most Holy Trinity – was built in 1832 and has strong ties with Magdelen College, Oxford, which gave the church two ancient doorways and a chantry. Sulhamstead Lock was another of the Trust's earliest rebuilding achievements using prison labour and army equipment. The tree-lined section up to Tyle Mill Lock (99) is classic Kennet valley countryside. Just below the lock is the first hand-operated swing bridge, which requires a windlass, and BW's first water point and Sanitary Station. About half a mile down the road to the north (at the junction with the A4) is Mulligans which describes itself as "The fresh fish and seafood experience". It was formerly the Three King's Jack's Booth pub and now serves excellent fish meals lunch time and evenings, booking is advisable (0118 930 2307).

Tyle Mill to Woolhampton

Ufton swing bridge requires a BW key and windlass. The de-gated Ufton Lock originally raised the level of the canal by 1ft 9in to the next lock (Towney) in the days when it was turf-sided. The Winning Hand by the A4, provides an excellent choice of food at lunchtime and in the evenings seven days a week (0118 9302472). At Towney Lock, beware of the top gate paddles which let in a deluge of water unless carefully controlled. Padworth Swing Bridge beyond is power-operated (BW key) and around the corner is the re-built Padworth Lock with its attractive landscaping and non-slip bricks! Beyond is Padworth Lower Wharf and its Visitor Centre in a former Lengthman's cottage. Adjacent are the premises of Reading Marine.

On the opposite bank are attractive half timbered private dwellings and a former Brewery.

The controls of Aldermaston Lift Bridge require a BW key for access and involve red flashing warning lights, bells and automatic barriers. The bridge should be operated by an adult. Note: The mechanism is automatically switched off between 8–9am and 4.30–5.30pm and during the hours of darkness. Locally produced timber, flour and malt were the main commodities handled from Aldermaston Wharf which the Great Western Railway extended to link up with their mainline via a spur to the north of the lock. There is a Sanitary Station and water point on the Wharf.

Basic groceries are available from the Elf Garage on the A4 trunk road (300 yards east from the junction with the A340) while, about 5 minutes walk further on, is the Courtyard Hotel and Restaurant, which welcomes non-residents, including children, to its restaurant for breakfast, lunch and dinner. (Bookings are advisable 0118 971 4411). Bar snacks are served from 10am to 10.30pm. A hundred yards south of the bridge is the Butt Inn (Whitbread) serving bar meals.

Aldermaston Lock, with its attractive 'scalloped' brickwork was re-opened in 1985 after two years of restoration under a Manpower Services Commission scheme. Salmon Cut takes the canal alongside the railway and under Frouds Bridge which replaced a swing span during restoration. The Rising Sun, a Free House serving bar snacks and restaurant meals, specialising in steaks ranging from huge to ordinary sizes, is half a mile north of the bridge on the A4 – book for Sat eve meals (0118 971 2717). Approached down the backwater towards Aldermaston Mill where corn used to be delivered by barge is the extensive Frouds Bridge Marina. Continuing up the main river, the navigation twists and turns through a delightfully wooded section and passing under the new Wickham Knights Bridge, one of the most bizarre 'up-and-over' bridges on the canal system! A folly it may be but it does allow disabled access as the towpath crosses to the south side.

Picture: Hugh Potter

The **power-operated bascule bridge** at **Aldermaston Wharf** dominates the scene and contrasts with traditional boating costumes.

Reading Marine 🛏 🛒 🚽 🍴 🛢

(0118 971 3666, www.readingmarine.com). Monday–Sat 8am to 5pm, Sunday in emergency. Narrowboats for hire, permanent moorings, pumpout, chandlery, solid fuel, boatbuilding, fitting out and repair, breakdown callout service craneage and brokerage.

Frouds Bridge Marina 🛏 🛒 🚽 🍴 🛢

(0118 971 4508) moorings, pump out, engine repairs, chandlery and solid fuels.

Woolhampton 🍴 🛒 🍺

Woolhampton Post Office and Village Stores (Mon–Sat 9am until 5pm, Sun until 12 midday) is on the main A4 together with two of three pubs – The Falmouth Arms (Eldridge Pope) which has B&B accomodation, and The Angel Inn (Whitbread). Both serve food – the Angel Inn has a restaurant – and guest beers. The third pub, by the swing bridge, is the Rowbarge, a free house with a selection of real ales, serving bar snacks, restaurant meals and with barbeques in summer. A collection of weapons, brass memorabilia and a conservatory, combine to make this friendly canalside pub well worth a visit – weekend booking for meals is advisable (0118 971 2213).

The swing bridge requires a BW key. Note: In order to keep approaches clear, mooring is not permitted either side of the bridge. It is recommended that you prepare the lock before taking your boat through the bridge passing directly between the mooring below the bridge and the lock or vice versa.

Bridges 31–42

Beware of cross-currents upstream of bridge 31. Oxlease and Cranwell, the next two swing bridges before and after Heale's Lock, require a windlass to release them. Approaching Midgham Lock, two pencil-like church spires enhance the landscape – Midgham (1869), in the style of the 14th century to the north, and Brimpton (of flint faced brick) to the south. On the A4, half a mile up the road from the lock, is The Coach & Horses (Wethereds), serving hot and cold food with real ale and a good selection of wines every day (except Sunday eves).

Thatcham 🚽 🗑 🛒 ♨ ⚙

The village centre lies about a mile north of Thatcham bridge, but it is not necessary to walk that distance if all your needs can be met in a chip shop, supermarket, chemist, Post Office, health centre or hairdressing salon, for all these are in Station Road at the Burwood Centre about 5 minutes walk from the canal (the Alldays supermarket and newspaper shop is open every day from 6–10pm). If you do venture into Thatcham, there are banks, a choice of four pubs, two Chinese and one Indian restaurant, a fish & chip shop and Gateways Supermarket. Of historical interest is St Mary's Church, with its fine 12th century Norman arch in the south porch, and in the town's square, a carved 13th century stone which is part of the Market Cross. The Swan (Courage), just beyond the level crossing, serves lunches Mon to Sat and eve meals Tue to Sat in the bar or restaurant (01635 862084).

Bridges 42–56

Beyond is Monkey Marsh Lock (90), which was supposed to have been re-built as a turf-sided lock but due to a design blunder has turned into a 'concrete-sided' lock, complete with steel walkways, unique in Britain! This lock together with the next one, Widmead, were opened in a special joint ceremony (just before H.M. The Queen declared the whole navigation open at Devizes), marking the completion of the Reading to Newbury section in July 1990.

Nature Reserves each side of the river section have been created around former gravel pits where there is good trout fishing and bird watching. Designated as a Site of Special Scientific Interest, the Thatcham Moors Reed Beds Reserve on the towpath side harbours warblers and similar species.

A short river section leads to Bull's Lock, which has a propensity for catching deep-draughted boats on its lower sill, particularly

Picture: Euan Corrie

A pair of narrowboats share Garston Lock, the only Kennet Navigation turf sided chamber to retain its original form after restoration, unlike Monkey Marsh which bears no resemblance to its original appearance.

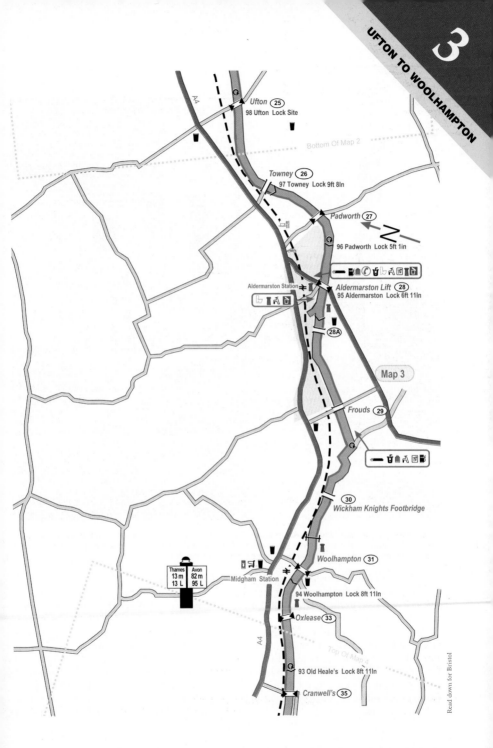

Ufton (25)
98 Ufton Lock Site

Bottom Of Map 2

Towney (26)
97 Towney Lock 9ft 8in

Padworth (27)
96 Padworth Lock 5ft 1in

Aldermarston Station _Aldermarston Lift_ (28)
95 Aldermarston Lock 6ft 11in

(28A)

Map 3

Frouds (29)

(30)
Wickham Knights Footbridge

Thames	Avon
13 m	82 m
13 L	95 L

Midgham Station _Woolhampton_ (31)

94 Woolhampton Lock 8ft 11in

Oxlease (33)

Top Of Map 4

93 Old Heale's Lock 8ft 11in

Cranwell's (35)

Picture: Peter Ivermee

The steerer keeps narrowboat *Nutfield* well off set as he heads downstream from the tail of Newbury Lock through the arch of the town bridge in order to counteract the strong current which funnels out though the towpath bridge to the left.

when the river level is down. Beware of cross currents and sand shoals at the entrance to the lock and keep to the centre of the channel. The swing bridge requires a windlass. From here to the centre of Newbury, the river and the canal alternate, passing through two locks – Ham Mills and Greenham – above which are the extensive facilities of the Newbury Boat Company, and passing by some of the town's modern industrial estates.

Newbury

All services. EC Wed. MD Thurs, Sat. Banks. Tourist Info at The Wharf (01635 30267). Launderette Queens Road. Newbury took its name from the Saxon village of Ulvritone soon after 1066 when a Norman Lord 'received' the land and was granted the right to hold fairs and markets. The town's prosperity however, had to wait until the 15th century, when the cloth industry flourished

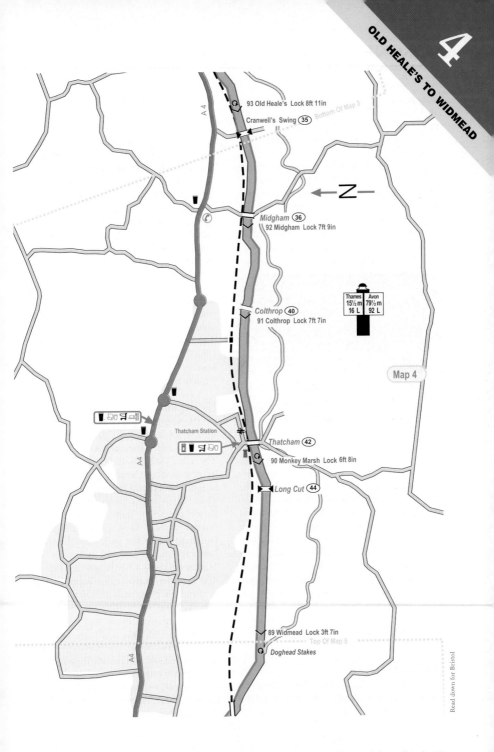

93 Old Heale's Lock 8ft 11in

Cranwell's Swing (35) Bottom Of Map 3

—N→

Midgham (36)
92 Midgham Lock 7ft 9in

Colthrop (40)
91 Colthrop Lock 7ft 7in

Thames	Avon
15½ m	79½ m
16 L	92 L

Map 4

Thatcham Station

Thatcham (42)
90 Monkey Marsh Lock 6ft 8in

Long Cut (44)

89 Widmead Lock 3ft 7in
Top Of Map 5
Doghead Stakes

A 4

Read down for Bristol

under such patriots as John Winchcombe, also known as Jack of Newbury, who at his peak was said to have owned 200 looms and to have employed 1000 men, women and children.

Two Civil Wars and the siege of nearby Donnington Castle followed and it was the river that helped to rescue the local economy. Once the Kennet Navigation opened in 1723, locally produced malt and barley were the main exports and coal was the major import. Today, Newbury is still influenced by com-

Picture: Euan Corrie

A memorial, at Newbury Lock, to one of the most determined campaigners for this waterway who fought for our future enjoyment of it for over half a century.

munications with the M4 and the nearby A34 trunk road linking the south coast ports with the Midlands. The shops are easily accessible from moorings on the wharf or from the towpath opposite. Disappointingly the substantial modern toilet building on the wharf has not been provided with an elsan disposal facility. Northbrook Street has departmental stores (including M&S), and off Bartholomew Street there is the Kennet Shopping Centre. If pork, ham, home-made sausages and pies take your fancy, do not miss Newbury's long established Sausage Manufacturers, Griffin Ltd, (closed Monday afternoon), on the south side of Newbury Bridge.

Places of interest

Newbury, or West Berkshire, Museum (across from the wharf) is housed in a 17th century Cloth Hall and 18th century

Granary. The Civil Wars are presented in audio-visual form and there are displays of local town life and industry through the ages ending with an exhibition of hot air ballooning, a popular local pastime. The Kennet Navigation's former terminus basin, between the wharf and the museum, is now occupied by a car park, and only the granary and a replica crane reminds us of the canal age (the granary is now the K&ACT Newbury branch HQ and museum). The town centre Parish Church of St Nicholas, completed in 1532 at the expense of John Winchcombe, has been radically Victorianised but includes some interesting features; the Perpendicular oak roof of the nave, the splendid pulpit of 1607, and many memorial tablets and brasses including those of its benefactor and his spouse. The 1861 Corn Exchange dominates the market square, where open markets are held every Thursday and Saturday.

Eating out

On the wharf are the Granary Tea Room and the Demoulin serving light lunches, real coffee and a wide range of teas and soft drinks. There are over twenty restaurants to choose from including Cantonese (August Moon), Indian (Ellora) and Italian (Deep Pan Pizza) all in Bartholomew Street close to the Rat & Parrot pub; the Valle D'Oro (Italian), in Oxford Street, Toby Grills' Robin Hood (English) across the park from the Wharf in London Road There are two pubs in the Market Square – Old Waggon & Horses and The Hatchet, both serving lunchtime meals only and the Hogshead in Wharf Street. The Tap & Spile in Northbrook Street offers snacks, vegetarian meals and Sunday roasts as well as real ale and the Dolphin in Bartholemew Street has Courage beers as well as guests and meals lunchtime and evening every day. Commanding a view of the lock from above the town bridge is the Lock Stock & Barrel offering food from 12 to 4pm daily and incorporating a coffee shop.

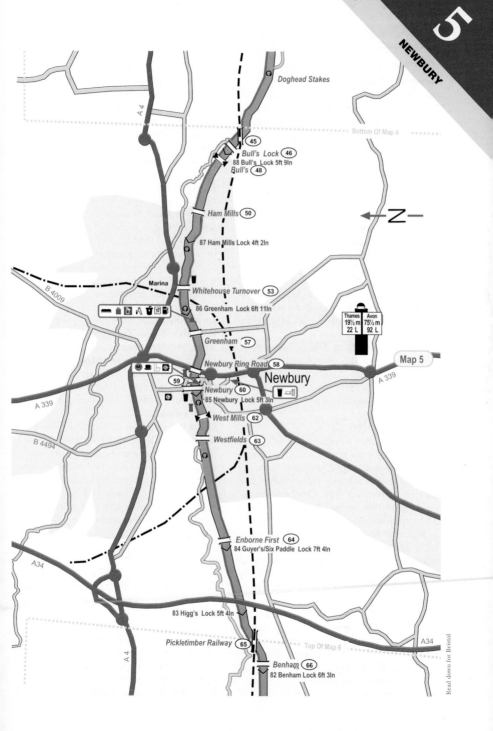

Doghead Stakes

A4

Bottom Of Map 4

45
Bull's Lock 46
88 Bull's Lock 5ft 9In
Bull's 48

Ham Mills 50

87 Ham Mills Lock 4ft 2In

Marina

B 4009

Whitehouse Turnover 53

86 Greenham Lock 6ft 11In

Thames   Avon
19½ m   75½ m
22 L   92 L

Greenham 57

Newbury Ring Road 58

Map 5

Newbury

A 339

59

A 339

Newbury 60

85 Newbury Lock 5ft 3In

B 4494

West Mills 62

Westfields 63

Enborne First 64

84 Guyer's/Six Paddle Lock 7ft 4In

83 Higg's Lock 5ft 4In

Pickletimber Railway 65

Top Of Map 6

A4

A34

Benham 66

82 Benham Lock 6ft 3In

Newbury Boat Co — 🏠 📷 🛢 ⚓
(01635 42884) Based at Greenham Lock, Moorings, including short term. All services, on Greenham island above the lock. Pump-out, Solid Fuel, Covered paint dock, craneage, repairs and refits. Also long term mooring at Ham Lock. Bryan Cotton (01635 49307) undertakes boat painting here.

All-Aboard Marine Services (01635 37606) also based at Greenham Lock offer engineering services and will look after your boat's systems such as plumbing and gas as well as offering a break down call out service.

Inland Waterway Holiday Cruises (07831 110811, www.bargeholiday.uk.com) are based with the Newbury Boat Co and operate a pair of traditional hotel narrow-boats throughout the inland waterway system carrying passengers in full board comfort.

Kennet Horse Boat Co 32 West Mills, Newbury, Berkshire RG14 5HU (01635 44154). Operate the diesel engined trip boat *Avon* from Newbury and horse drawn *Kennet Valley* from Kintbury.

Bridges 58–75

Newbury has two notable canal bridges – Parkway Bridge (above the wharf), a temporary war-time structure has been noted for its restricted headroom particularly when the river is running high. Complete reconstruction of this bridge was undertaken in 2001 to provide clearance of 2.6m (8ft 6in) at normal river level. The second is Newbury Town Bridge (circa 1770), with its elegant span and balustrades. Beware of the strong cross current between the bridge and the lock which has been made more severe by recent towpath alterations. Beyond is Newbury Lock, with its rare lever-operated ground paddles, usually padlocked out of use, and West Mills Swing Bridge, which requires a BW key and windlass. The pink painted canalside dwellings after the bridge were once weavers' cottages.

Heading west, the navigation leaves the river at Northcroft Fields and the canal takes the voyager past the bridge abutments of the long-since closed Lambourn Valley Railway and into Guyers Lock. Continuing westwards, the canal passes through some beautiful scenery. It is also crossed by the A34 bypass, the construction of which, through nearby woodlands, caused much controversy. Before these works the green and wooded backdrops created by Enborne Copse, Hamstead and Benham Parks, More Wood and Irish Copse embodied the very quintessence of our English countryside as well as providing some wonderful lock settings. Along the way are Pickletimber Railway Bridge (so called after its wooden forebear), Benham Wide (created to appease the aesthetic sensibilities of Lord Craven) and Inkpen Beacons just visible to the south of Drewett's Lock. The river Kennet, meanwhile, provides deep water for the boater in the canalised sections one moment and bubbling shallows and quiet pools for the fly fisherman the next, as it tumbles over weirs and creates some of the best fly fishing beats in Berkshire.

Half a mile north of Hamstead Bridge is the thatched hamlet of Marsh Benham. There is much hot air ballooning in this area culminating in the annual Icicle Balloon Meeting nearby in January. At Shepherds Bridge, the track leading up Irish Hill to the south rewards the climber with fine views over the Kennet Valley and southwards to Inkpen and Ham Hill.

Kintbury 🛢 ⚙ 🛏 🍺

Kintbury is a quiet village which boasted three watermills and a silk mill in the early 19th century. Shopping needs are well catered for with a butcher, baker, newsagent, corner store, off-licence and tea shop, all at the top of the hill. The Dundas Arms (Morlands), named after the first chairman of the Canal Company, overlooks the lock entrance, offers accomodation and boasts an Egon Ronay recommended restaurant and

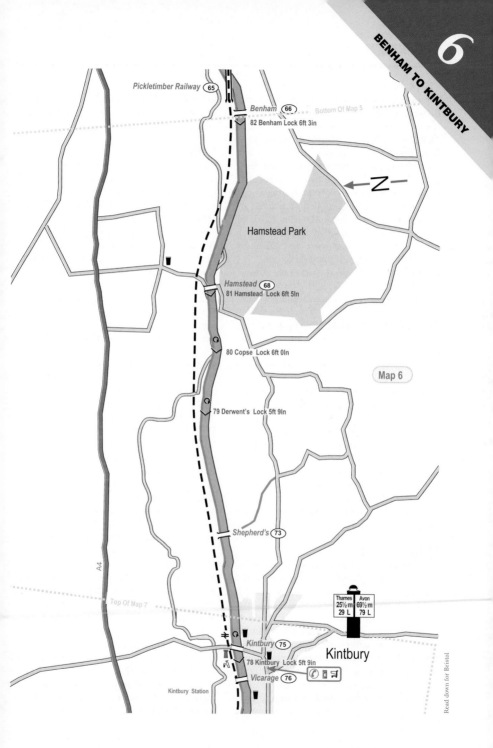

Pickletimber Railway ⑥⑤

Benham ⑥⑥   Bottom Of Map 5
82 Benham Lock 6ft 3in

← N ─

Hamstead Park

Hamstead ⑥⑧
81 Hamstead Lock 6ft 5In

80 Copse Lock 6ft 0In

Map 6

79 Derwent's Lock 5ft 9In

Shepherd's ⑦③

Top Of Map 7

Thames	Avon
25½ m	69½ m
29 L	79 L

Kintbury ⑦⑤

Kintbury

78 Kintbury Lock 5ft 9in

Vicarage ⑦⑥

Kintbury Station

Read down for Bristol

bar food (except Mon evenings and Sun). Booking is advised for Fridays or Saturdays (01488 658263). The Prince of Wales (Archers) in Newbury Street (first left turn from bridge) is a friendly pub serving bar food and a roast on Sundays. The Blue Ball, at the top of the High Street serves bar snacks and is open all day on Saturdays.

Kintbury's old wharf handled all manner of goods, mainly coal, iron ore, watercress and whiting, a locally quarried chalk that was processed to a fine powder and taken by barge to Bristol's paint manufacturers. **Kennet Horse Boat Co** (see under Newbury, above) operates the horse drawn trip boat *Kennet Valley* from Kintbury.

Bridges 76–83. Leaving Kintbury,

the canal passes the Parish Church, which dates back to the 13th century, and its elegant Victorian vicarage. Look out for Avington village with its Norman Church between Brunsden and Wire locks to the north. Intercity 125 trains roar alongside before crossing over from one side of the canal to the other. On the approach to Hungerford, the Kennet makes its final bow at Dunn Mill. Water meadows and a trout farm feature here and at one point, the canal and river are separated only by the towpath. A Sanitary Station, water point and winding hole are located by the footbridge which leads to the station.

Hungerford

All Services. MD Wed. Launderette in the High Street. Richard I granted the town's seal and John O'Gaunt gave it fishing rights on the Kennet, exacting a nominal rent of a single rose! The High Street, with its mixture of 17th and 18th century buildings, is where the shops are and where the annual Hocktide Ceremony is held on the second Tuesday after Easter. It is about 'electing' 99 Burgesses, Commoners' rights and Tuttimen who exercise their right to collect a 'headpenny' and to receive a kiss, from all the ladies of every house which enjoys Commoner's rights, in return for an orange!

Eating out
The Bear Hotel (01488 682512 www.thebearathungerford.co.uk) at the junction with the A4 trunk road, boasts 13th century origins, ownership by two of Henry VIII's queens and, as a coaching stage and post house on the London to Bath Road, playing host to Queen Elizabeth I and William of Orange. Bookings for lunch or dinner in its Brasserie David Cecil are advisable (01488 685327), bar snacks are served in the Courtyard Bar. Other eating places include the Tutti Pole Tea Shop by the canal bridge and the Hoowah Chinese restaurant. Pubs are numerous with The Lamb (Courage) and The Sun (Morlands) on the A4, The John O'Gaunt Inn (Morlands), which serves bar meals and has a restaurant and accommodation The Three Swans (Free House) and The Plume of Feathers (Greene King & Wadworth) in the High Street. Those needing some exercise may seek out the highly recommended Down Gate at the edge of Hungerford Common which serves Arkells beers and food at lunch times and every evening except Sundays and Mondays. Booking for Sunday roast lunch is advisable (01488 682708).

The town is also noted for its antique shops. St Lawrence's Church (circa 1816) beside the canal above Hungerford Lock, is noted for its Bath stone construction (the material was delivered by canal) and attendant swing bridge. The wharf area, where only a converted stone granary survives, offers limited mooring space, so doubling-up may be necessary, unless you tie up above the lock.

Rose of Hungerford. (01488 683389). Public and charter boat trips from Hungerford Wharf.

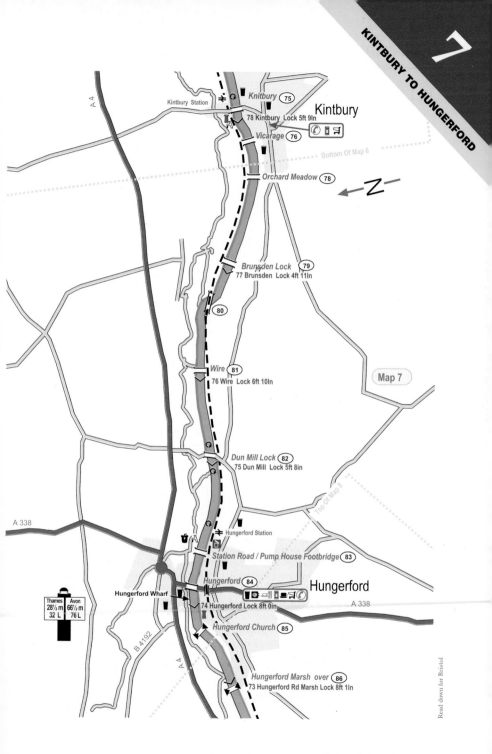

Kintbury Station

Knitbury ⑦⑤

Kintbury

78 Kintbury Lock 5ft 9ln

Vicarage ⑦⑥

Bottom Of Map 6

Orchard Meadow ⑦⑧

←–N–

Brunsden Lock ⑦⑨
77 Brunsden Lock 4ft 11ln

⑧⑩

Wire ⑧①
76 Wire Lock 6ft 10ln

Map 7

Dun Mill Lock ⑧②
75 Dun Mill Lock 5ft 8in

Top Of Map 8

Hungerford Station

Station Road / Pump House Footbridge ⑧③

Hungerford ⑧④

Hungerford Wharf

Hungerford

A 338

74 Hungerford Lock 8ft 0in

Thames	Avon
28½ m	66½ m
32 L	76 L

Hungerford Church ⑧⑤

Hungerford Marsh over ⑧⑥
73 Hungerford Rd Marsh Lock 8ft 1ln

Read down for Bristol

Kennet & Avon Canal 33

Bridges 84–95

Open common land leads up to Hungerford Marsh Lock which, surprisingly, has a swing bridge astride its chamber. The story goes that, during the building of the canal, the engineers chose to ignore the presence of a right of way until after the lock was built, when the commoners exercised their rights!

Note: Swing the bridge clear before locking up or down.

From above Cobbler's Lock to the summit the canal and railway are inseparable. Both continue to climb, crossing the river Dun (don't miss the Dun aqueduct above Cobbler's Lock) and the Berkshire/Wiltshire border at Froxfield Bridge. Beyond the bridge was Froxfield Wharf (where the winding hole now is) and Froxfield Feeder, which feeds about half the stream's flow into the canal via a circular weir. The other half disappears down a culvert and originally supplemented supplies to Oakhill Mill.

On the A4 Bath Road in Froxfield half a mile from the bridge is The Pelican Inn (free house with Fullers' beers) serving food at lunchtimes and evenings throughout the week with a special Sunday lunch (for which book on 01488 682479) accompanied by Jazz. There is an adventure playground and some sizeable trout to view in a tributary of the Dun which runs through the garden.

The canal climbs the two Froxfield Locks and Oakhill Down Lock, before arriving at Little Bedwyn. Bisected by the canal and the railway, the north side of the village has a row of 19th century houses running up to the church while on the south side. About 300 yards south from the pedestrian bridge is the Harrow Inn (01672 870871 www.harrowinn.co.uk). This pub, once owned by the villagers themselves now operates as a restaurant. It has no draught beers but offers bottled 6X, and an excellent choice of wine to accompany your meal. It is open Thur–Sat for dinner, and Tue–Sat lunch, but closed Sun night and all day Mon. in fine weather you may dine on the terrace.

At lock 65, there is evidence of a former swing bridge astride the lock chamber. At Great Bedwyn Wharf however, there is no evidence of the two coal merchants who once traded there, only a Sanitary Station and elsan disposal and a water point. There is a winding hole above the wharf and owners of full length craft should be aware that this is the last turning point before the summit – the winding hole below Crofton Pumping Station is for craft up to 50ft maximum.

Southern Boat Services (01672 870158) operate permanent moorings at Great Bedwyn Wharf.

The Bruce Trust, PO Box 21, Hungerford, Berkshire RG17 9YY (01672 515498 www.brucetrust.org.uk) operates wide beam boats specially fitted out for self drive hire by groups or families including disabled people or any who have problems with mobility. The boats are based at Foxhanger and Great Bedwyn wharves.

Great Bedwyn ▮ ⓒ ⊟ ▯ Ⓜ

Five minutes walk from the wharf is Great Bedwyn village, where there is a village store, off-licence, a bakery and a Post Office (on the road towards Crofton. The Three Tuns (real Fullers and Flowers beers) at the top of the hill likes to be described as "a pub that serves food not a restaurant with beer" and serves bar snacks and restaurant meals (Mon–Sat) while The Cross Keys (Wiltshire Brewery) at the cross roads does the same (7 days a week). The parish church of St Mary Virgin, with its unusual crossing tower, dates back to the 12th century, while the Bedwyn Stone Museum (01672 870234) in the same road, adjacent to the Post Office,

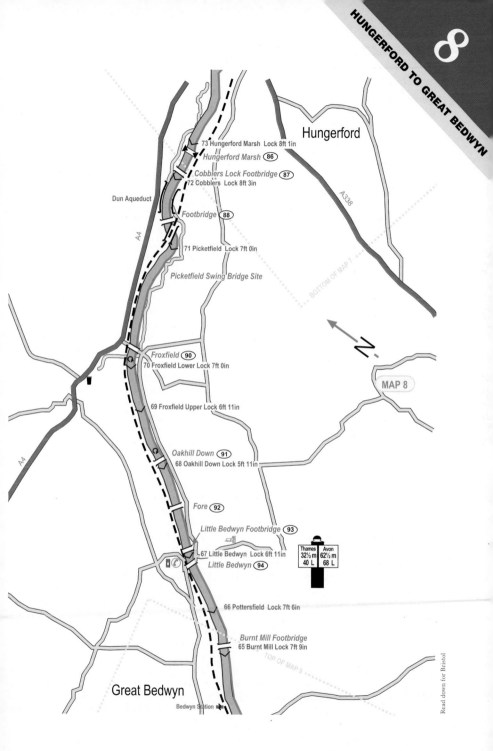

Hungerford

73 Hungerford Marsh Lock 8ft 1in
Hungerford Marsh (86)
Cobblers Lock Footbridge (87)
72 Cobblers Lock 8ft 3in

Dun Aqueduct

Footbridge (88)

71 Picketfield Lock 7ft 0in

Picketfield Swing Bridge Site

Froxfield (90)
70 Froxfield Lower Lock 7ft 0in

69 Froxfield Upper Lock 6ft 11in

Oakhill Down (91)
68 Oakhill Down Lock 5ft 11in

Fore (92)

Little Bedwyn Footbridge (93)
67 Little Bedwyn Lock 6ft 11in
Little Bedwyn (94)

Thames	Avon
32½ m	62½ m
40 L	68 L

66 Pottersfield Lock 7ft 6in

Burnt Mill Footbridge
65 Burnt Mill Lock 7ft 9in

Great Bedwyn

Bedwyn Station

A4

A338

BOTTOM OF MAP 7

MAP 8

TOP OF MAP 9

Read down for Bristol

exhibits the work of seven generations (the Lloyd family made the tableture above the east portal of Bruce Tunnel). The museum is open daily and well worth a visit which may include the chance to watch work in progress.

Bridge 96–Bruce Tunnel

The railway and canal continue side by side as they head west through ever encroaching wooded hillsides towards Crofton. At Crofton Bridge, a Roman road passes overhead before the engine house pound and Crofton Pumping Station are reached.

Crofton Pumping Station

The imposing brick building houses two early 19th century beam engines whose job it was to raise water 40ft up from Wilton Water opposite and discharge it into the summit level of the canal via a mile-long feeder. Electric pumps do the job today, but the beam engines have been restored by the Trust and are open to visitors daily (static) from Easter to the end of September, and in steam on Bank Holiday weekends and the last weekends of January, July and September (01672 80300).

The earliest of the two engines – an 1812 Boulton & Watt – is the oldest working beam engine in the world still in its original building and doing its original job. Wilton Water, which is the only source of supply for the summit, is man-made and spring-fed; it is also a haven for waterfowl, wildlife and fish. Wilton Windmill, which can be reached on foot 1.5 miles south of Crofton Bridge, is the oldest working windmill in Wessex; open every Sunday and Bank Holiday afternoons 2–5pm Easter to the end of September, (01672 870427).

There are nine locks in the Crofton Flight taking the canal to its summit level at 450ft above sea level; 35 miles and 52 locks from Kennet Mouth at Reading.

The 2.5 mile summit starts with a winding hole, the feeder entry from Crofton's pumps and the bridge abutments of the former Swindon, Marlborough & Andover Railway of 1882.

Bruce Tunnel–Bridge 108

Wooded cuttings either side of Bruce Tunnel (the only tunnel on the canal) give a feeling of remoteness, but at the time of its opening in 1810, when Thomas Bruce, Earl of Ailesbury performed the ceremony, there was much activity and celebration. The inscribed tablet above the eastern portal acknowledges the Earl's . . .'uniform and effectual support'. The brick lined 502-yard tunnel has no towpath, and as the horses were led over the hill, crews hauled their barges through by hand using chains attached to the south wall.

Beyond the tunnel, the canal touches the edge of Savernake Forest before passing under Burbage Bridge, a fine example of a skew bridge. At Burbage Wharf is a replica wooden crane to one of John Rennie's designs; the wharf buildings, which are leased from The Crown Estates, have been restored for residential use. Meanwhile, the railway has crossed from the north side to the south above the tunnel. Martinsell Hill to the north dominates the scenery here while four locks take the canal down to Wootton Rivers, passing Brimslade Farm and on to the 15 mile 'Long Pound'.

Wootton Rivers 🍺 🄯

Thatched roofs dominate the houses in Wootton Rivers, including The Royal Oak, a 16th Century (Free House) pub serving meals at the bar and in an excellent restaurant 7 days a week – restaurant bookings at week-ends are advisable (01672 810322). The 13th Century St Andrew's Church has a curious clock which was built to commemorate the Coronation of George V in 1911. It was put

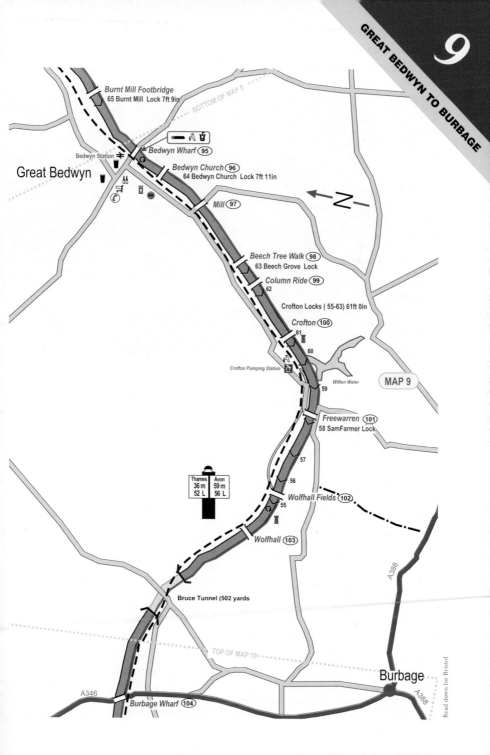

Burnt Mill Footbridge
65 Burnt Mill Lock 7ft 9in

BOTTOM OF MAP 8

Bedwyn Wharf (95)

Bedwyn Station

Great Bedwyn

Bedwyn Church (96)
64 Bedwyn Church Lock 7ft 11in

Mill (97)

←N—

Beech Tree Walk (98)
63 Beech Grove Lock

Column Ride (99)
62

Crofton Locks (55-63) 61ft 0in

Crofton (100)
61

60

Crofton Pumping Station

Wilton Water

MAP 9

59

Freewarren (101)
58 SamFarmer Lock

57

Thames	Avon
36 m	59 m
52 L	56 L

56

Wolfhall Fields (102)

55

Wolfhall (103)

Bruce Tunnel (502 yards

TOP OF MAP 10

A388

Burbage

Read down for Bristol

A346

Burbage Wharf (104)

A388

Picture: Alan Barnes

An ideal mooring for a visit to Crofton Pumping Station.

together by villager Jack Spratt from all kinds of locally donated pieces of scrap metal. It has a unique face, inscribed 'Glory to God', and strikes a different quarterly chime in 6-hourly cycles.

Bridges 109–114

The Long Pound is a 15 mile lock-free ribbon of water brilliantly engineered by John Rennie through the heart of Wiltshire. He carefully followed the contours and where necessary carved cuttings and built embankments to maintain the level to Devizes. The remoteness and largely undisturbed habitat for plant and bird life and the diversity of countryside as the waterway threads its way through the Vale of Pewsey enriches the eye and gladdens the heart! From a practical point of view however, the only water supply is from the summit which in turn relies upon supplies drawn from Wilton Water. The Long Pound is the only source of supply to the 29 locks at Caen Hill, so it is easy to understand the need to conserve every

drop of water and for the BW restrictions imposed on passage up and down the Devizes flight. Back pumps installed in a new building at Lower Foxhangers are used to return lockage water to two points in the flight or to the long pound as required.

The Waterfront, recently established at Pewsey Wharf provides a warm welcome. Moorings and services for passing boats are provided as well as day boat and canoe hire. Located nearly a mile above the town, the wharf is the focal point of a canal settlement of cottages, a manor house, and the French Horn pub (Wadworth) (01672 62443) reputedly named after a horn used to summon French prisoners working along the canal! Bar snacks and wholesome meals are available at lunchtimes and in the evening.

Pewsey

Pewsey provides all shopping needs, a bank (Lloyds), plus Calor Gas and coal from Wootton's in North Street who also

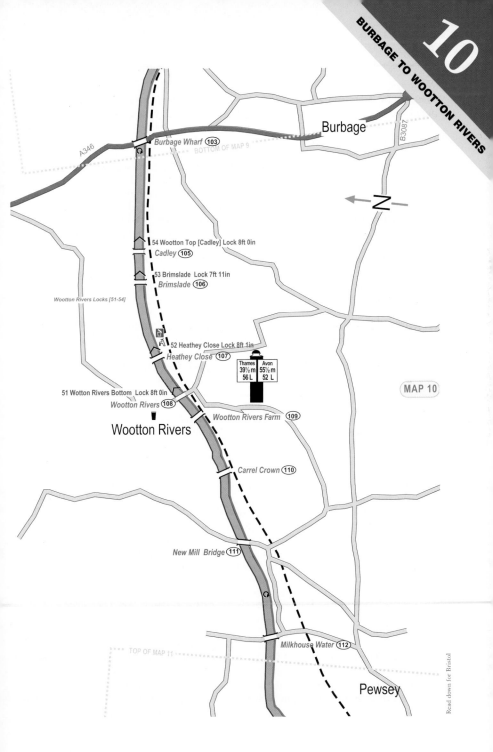

Burbage

A346

Burbage Wharf (103)
BOTTOM OF MAP 9

N

54 Wootton Top [Cadley] Lock 8ft 0in
Cadley (105)

53 Brimslade Lock 7ft 11in
Brimslade (106)

Wootton Rivers Locks [51-54]

52 Heathey Close Lock 8ft 1in
Heathey Close (107)

Thames	Avon
39½ m	55½ m
56 L	52 L

51 Wootton Rivers Bottom Lock 8ft 0in
Wootton Rivers (108)

Wootton Rivers

Wootton Rivers Farm (109)

MAP 10

Carrel Crown (110)

New Mill Bridge (111)

TOP OF MAP 11

Milkhouse Water (112)

Pewsey

B3087

Read down for Bristol

stock useful tools and materials for boat maintenance. There are no restaurants as such, but pub food is available at the Royal Oak (Wadworth), The Greyhound (Courage), The Phoenix (Whitbread) – all in the town centre – and The Coopers Arms (Free House) in Ball Road at the top end of the High Street.

The Waterfront ⌂ ⛴ ▣ ⬛ Ⓒ ⬮

At Pewsey Wharf, moorings, pump out, and slipway, day hire boats, canoe sales & hire, canalware and souvenirs.

Pewsey Vale Charter Cruises
(01703 266200). Public boat trips.

Bridges 114–124

Continuing westwards through Wilcot, the canal passes under two bridges of note - an iron suspension bridge linking Stowell Park with the village (made in Bath and utilising jointed iron bars rather than cables), and Lady's Bridge, an ornamental but elegant edifice built in 1808 to appease Lady Wroughton. She did not like the idea of a commercial waterway passing through her land and persuaded the canal company to create an artificial lake leading up to the bridge – Wilcot Wide – to disguise the true purpose of the waterway.

The Golden Swan (Wadworth) south of Wilcot Bridge, beyond the green, has the steepest pitched thatched roof in Wiltshire. It is a friendly pub with food throughout the week except Mon and Sun eves (01672 562289). Holy Cross Church, dating back to the 12th Century, is down the road to the right of the pub. Three quarters of a mile south of Ladies Bridge, is Swanborough Tump, a grassy knoll where tradition has it King Alfred held a Parliament. Thereafter a 'Court' was supposed to meet there annually and, amongst other things, report on the number of ash trees growing there; today there are three!

Cherry Craft (01747 850449, www.Cherrycraft.co.uk), operate permanent moorings and boat sales at Lady's Bridge.

Two hills dominate the northern landscape - Picked Hill, with its tuft of trees, and Woodborough Hill, with its ancient lynchet strips (field markings) to the south are sweeping vistas towards Salisbury Plain. The village of Honeystreet grew up around the canal and it was at the wharf west of the bridge that Robbins, Lane & Pinnegar built barges which they launched sideways into the canal.

Gibson's Boat Services ▤ ⬛ ⌂ ⛴

(01672 851232), Moorings (including short term). Services available (by appointment in winter) include Solid Fuel and surveys.

Bridge 124 The Barge Inn (Wadworth) beyond was more than a pub in the canal's heyday – it also had its own slaughter house and bakery. It was rebuilt after a disastrous fire in 1858 and its importance is indicated by the fact that it had 24 rooms and 15 fireplaces. Today, it provides a wide choice of meals all week, a games room, a live band on Fridays, a payphone and a water point. It is a choice spot to moor with fine views across to the Milk Hill White Horse, which dates back to 1812, and is popular with those interested in the nearby crop circles.

Alton Barnes Ⓒ The villages of Alton Barnes and Alton Priors are separated by a tree-lined brook. Both are well worth a visit if only to view a typical English farming community and two fine churches. St Marys, Alton Barnes, is an Anglo Saxon church in miniature with everything scaled down to the tiny proportions of the building. The isolated church of All Saints

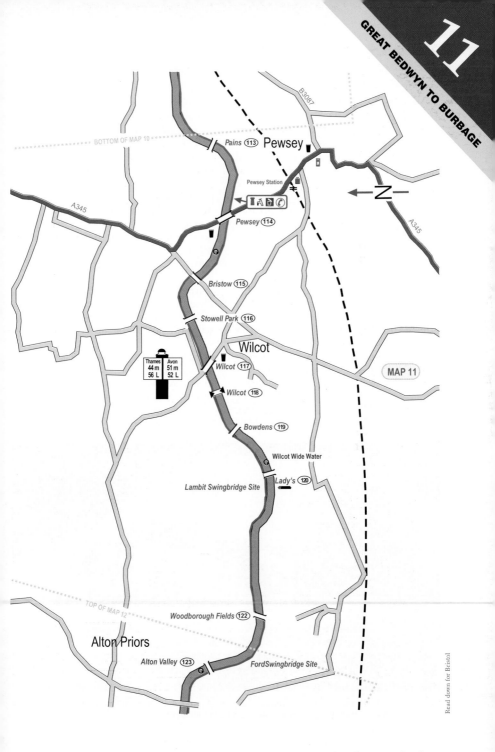

BOTTOM OF MAP 10

Pains ⑪③ Pewsey

B3087

A345

Pewsey Station

Pewsey ⑪④

Bristow ⑪⑤

Stowell Park ⑪⑥

A345

Wilcot

Thames | Avon
44 m | 51 m
56 L | 52 L

Wilcot ⑪⑦

MAP 11

Wilcot ⑪⑧

Bowdens ⑪⑨

Wilcot Wide Water

Lambit Swingbridge Site   Lady's ⑫⓪

TOP OF MAP 12

Woodborough Fields ⑫②

Alton Priors

Alton Valley ⑫③   FordSwingbridge Site

Read down for Bristol

at Alton Priors is approached across a field from its neighbour. Designated a redundant church, it is possible to gain access by borrowing the key from the first house to the north-east. Perpendicular in style, it has a wide nave and most unusual box tomb complete with Dutch brass plate. To the south east of the village runs The Ridgeway, a trade route between Streatley in Berkshire and Salisbury which dates from the Bronze Age.

Bridges 125–140

The canal continues its journey as richly as before through open countryside to the south, while a band of hills keeps watch as the waterway follows its circuitous route around, but not touching, the villages of Stanton St Bernard; All Cannings (post office/shop and off licence open 8–6pm Mon–Sat, Sun till 12.0, and The King's Arms (Wadworth) cold snacks; closed Mondays and Tuesdays); Horton, (The Bridge Inn (Wadworth) canalside with moorings, serving bar snacks); or Bishops Canning, (shop, gas, newspapers, open 9–4pm weekdays, Sun 9-1pm and The Crown (Wadworth) (01380 86218) bar snacks and restaurant meals. Bishops Canning church is a gem, being entirely Early English with a magnificent central tower and spire; inside is a 17th century penitential seat.

Allington has a hand-operated swing bridge requiring a BW key to release the holding bolt. That at Horton requires a windlass.

Between Laywood Bridge and Coate Road Bridge on the north bank is a major commercial and residential development, Waterbrook Mews, centred around Devizes Marina. A tree-lined cutting with several handsome stone bridges, including London Road Bridge at a right-angled turn, and an assortment of large houses overlooking the waterway leads the canal to Devizes Wharf where all services are available except pump-out.

Mooring space at the wharf is limited, which means doubling-up at peak periods.

Picture: Euan Corrie

Little remains at the former Robbins Lane & Pinnegar boat building yard to recall the substantial Honeystreet barges once built and maintained there.

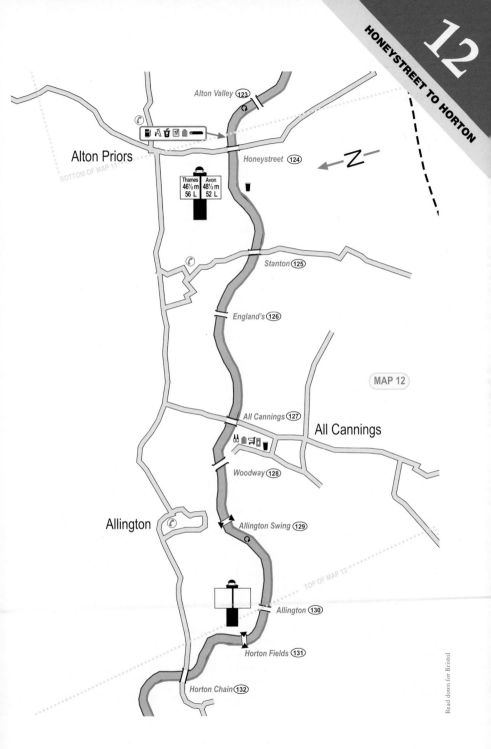

Alton Valley ⑫③

Alton Priors

BOTTOM OF MAP 11

Thames 46½ m 56 L	Avon 48½ m 52 L

Honeystreet ⑫④

Stanton ⑫⑤

England's ⑫⑥

MAP 12

All Cannings ⑫⑦

All Cannings

Woodway ⑫⑧

Allington

Allington Swing ⑫⑨

TOP OF MAP 13

Allington ⑬⓪

Horton Fields ⑬①

Horton Chain ⑬②

Read down for Bristol

Devizes Marina — ⏚ ⛴ ⛽

At the edge of the town between bridges 135 and 136. (01380 725300 www.devizesmarina.atfreeweb.com). Moorings, pump out, chandlery, solid fuel, wet dock, slipway, cranage, engine and boat repairs, breakdown service, boat sales and day boat hire.

Devizes

All Services. EC Wed. MD Thurs & Sat. Launderette (Market Place). Tourist Info in the Market Place (01380 729408) includes displays of Devizes' Medieval history. The origin of the name Devizes is associated with the town's first castle which was built on the boundary between the ancient manors of Bishops Cannings and Potterne in 1080. The Latin for 'on the boundaries' is Ad Divisas. The present 19th century castle is the third one on the site and is privately owned. From earliest times, Devizes has been a market town, with wool dominating trade from the 14th to the 18th century, as reflected in many of the town's splendid merchants houses. Anstie's Tobacco & Snuff business was founded in 1698, and was England's oldest until finally closing its doors in 1961. Brewing in Devizes began in 1786 and today is carried on by Wadworth & Co from their canalside premises beyond the wharf.

Places of interest

The Market Place (which is undergoing refurbishment at the time of writing) is the largest in the West of England, where the town's 1857 Corn Exchange stands alongside the 16th century Bear Hotel (once home of portrait painter Thomas Lawrence). The Market Cross recounts the story of Ruth Pierce, whom the Almighty struck down dead after she lied about paying for some wheat! The Town Hall was built in 1806, and close by is St John's Alley, an outstanding example of timber framing with a Jacobean upper floor. St John's Church, with its impressive crossing tower, is 12th century, and so is St Mary's, although much of it was rebuilt in the 15th century. Devizes Museum in Long Street houses treasures from the Neolithic, Bronze and Iron Ages, and charts the history of Wiltshire's henge monuments at Stonehenge, Avebury and Woodhenge. Upstairs are delightful displays of latter-day history, including an iron cello made by the local blacksmith in Milton Lilbourne which was played in the church in the years before the organ was installed in 1897. In addition there is an art gallery and archive. The museum is open from 10am to 5pm Mondays to Saturdays.

Pubs and Eating Out

Close to the wharf in Couch Lane is Wharfside Food & Crafts (01380 726051) offering country house style cooking on the premises. Pubs abound and most serve food – including The Bear Hotel (Wadworth) in the Market Place serving restaurant and bar meals, The Royal Oak (Ushers) and The Castle Hotel (Wadworth) in New Park Street, The Black Swan Hotel (Wadworth) in Northgate Street, The White Bear (Wadworth), in Monday Market Street, and The Artichoke (Wadworth) beyond Devizes Town Bridge, which also has B&B accommodation. Restaurants include The Grapevine Wine Bar & Restaurant in the High Street (lunches Mon–Sat, dinner Tues-Sat), Franco Ristorante in Swan Yard off the High Street (lunch and dinner Mon–Sat), there are also Indian and Chinese take-aways.

If Shire horses are of interest, Wadworth's stables close to Town Bridge are well worth a visit and are open 2–4pm on Tuesdays and Thursdays. Brewery Tours may be available by arrangement (01380723361, www.wadworth.co.uk)

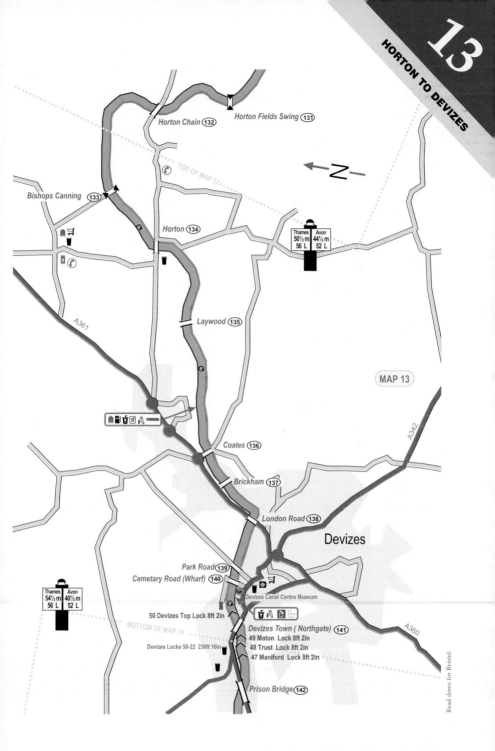

Horton Fields Swing (131)

Horton Chain (132)

TOP OF MAP 12

Bishops Canning (133)

Horton (134)

Thames	Avon
50½ m	44½ m
56 L	52 L

A361

Laywood (135)

MAP 13

A342

Coates (136)

Brickham (137)

London Road (138)

Devizes

Park Road (139)

Cemetary Road (Wharf) (140)

Devizes Canal Centre Museum

Thames	Avon
54½ m	40½ m
56 L	52 L

BOTTOM OF MAP 14

50 Devizes Top Lock 8ft 2in

Devizes Town (Northgate) (141)

49 Maton Lock 8ft 2in

48 Trust Lock 8ft 2in

Devizes Locks 50-22 236ft 10in

47 Maniford Lock 8ft 2in

Prison Bridge (142)

Read down for Bristol

A360

Devizes to Westminster Canoe Race

This annual event, which commenced in 1947, takes place over the Easter period. It extends from Park Road Bridge to the steps at County Hall, Westminster. There are 77 locks around which canoes must be portaged and 120 miles to cover including a tidal section into London on the Thames. There are over 300 entries each year.

Devizes Wharf 🏕 ⛴ 🅱 🛉

The town had three wharves – Sussex Wharf below Town Bridge, Lower Wharf above Lock 50 and Town Wharf which survives today. Good use is made of the two restored wharf buildings – one houses the Wharf Theatre, the town's only permanent live theatre with around eight productions a year, (0672 721850), whilst the other – the long building hugging the south side – is home for the Kennet & Avon Canal Trust's offices, shop, meeting room and Museum. The shop and museum are open from 10am to 4.30pm from February until Christmas (01380 721489). A few yards towards the town is Wharfside, a collection of shops and a chandlery. There is a BW water point, elsan and rubbish disposal and toilet on the wharf.

Wharfside Chandlery (01380 725007). Chandlery and gifts.

White Horse Boats (01380 828043). Boats for day, short term and weekly hire from Devizes Wharf, Trip Boat, Pump-out, Boat fitting and repairs.

Diesel & Marine Engineering Services (01380 722962 or 07973 859988) Tim Stevens provides mobile engineering services, anywhere between Newbury and Bath, for all the systems on all types of boat including gas, diesel, heating, water and engine repairs as well as carrying out safety scheme work.

Bridges 140–146 The Devizes flight of 29 locks can be divided into three groups – the first six from Town Bridge to Lock 45, the 17 Caen Hill locks with their regular formation and attendant side ponds, and the remaining six locks which take the canal down to Lower Foxhangers. (See under Devizes Flight on page 4) The engineering achievement is spectacular – a climb of 234ft in just over two miles using 29 locks and an ingenious layout of widened pounds. It clearly is one of the Wonders of the Waterways.

Four to six hours should be allowed for the flight and remember to have a film in your camera to capture the Caen Hill locks and the sweeping landscapes on the descent. Between locks 47 and 48 is Wadworth's Black Horse pub (real ale and meals), opposite which is a garden centre with coffee shop; while on the west side of the Bath Road Bridge is a carved stone plaque acknowledging John Blackwell's 34 years work as the canal company's Superintendent, duties which he performed with 'fidelity, vigilance and ability', circa 1840. At lock 44 is BW's Waterway Manager's office and depot. With team work the locks are accomplished without a break. West of lock 26 was a gas works which provided lighting for the locks enabling round-the-clock use. At Lower Foxhangers is a BW water point and Sanitary Station, moorings, a slipway and the remains of piers which supported the Devizes branch of the Wilts, Somerset & Weymouth Railway line.

Foxhangers Wharf 🏕 🅱 🏬

(01380 828254, www.foxhangers.co.uk). Moorings. Slipway. Pump out. B&B, camping and self catering holiday accommodation.

Foxhanger Canal Holidays (01380 828795 www.foxhangers.co.uk). Craft for hire by the week with short breaks occasionally available at short notice.

Picture: British Waterways

By far the best viewpoint from which to appreciate the Caen Hill flight! The town of Devizes occupies the extreme top right and BW's offices and maintenance yard overlook the sideponds from the top centre.

Nelcris Marine (01380 828807). Repair and call-out service.

The Bruce Trust PO Box 21, Hungerford, Berkshire RG17 9YY (01672 515498 www.brucetrust.org.uk) operates wide beam boats specially fitted out for self drive hire by groups or families including disabled people or any who have problems with mobility. The boats are based at Foxhanger and Great Bedwyn wharves.

Devizes Narrowboat Builders also at Foxhangers Wharf (01380 828848) fit out narrowboat shells whether obtained through themselves or elsewhere and also offer repair services.

Bridges 146–151

Continuing westwards, the canal crosses Summerham Brook which feeds into the canal about half a mile on by Martinslade Wharf. For sustenance, the Three Magpies (Wadworth) a quarter of a mile north of Sells Green bridge has a restaurant which is open every day, and there is a UK filling station close by in case diesel or petrol are required.

Seend ⌐ ▯ ▮

Hills to the south leading up to Seend village contrast with pastoral landscapes to the north, whilst on the canal, two swing bridges, requiring a BW windlass to unlock, provide a warm-up for the first of Seend's five locks. The Post Office stores in the High Street at the top of the hill on the A361 (15 mins walk from the top lock) provide the full range of groceries (closed Sat pm and all day Sun. At the other end of the High Street The Bell Inn (Wadworth) serves hot food Mon–Friday (except Monday evenings).

At Lock 19 in the adjoining field to the south are the remains of Seend Iron Works; ore was smelted here in two blast furnaces for 30 years. Little remains also of Seend wharf below the lock, except for a stone building, but the situation is saved by the presence of the Barge Inn (Wadworth), a lively canalside pub with moorings and an excellent menu to suit all tastes – food served all week including Sunday lunchtimes and eves (01380 828230). The village of Seend Cleeve to the south supports the Brewery Inn (Smiles), five minutes up the hill past Ferrum Towers, formerly the Iron Master's house. The Brewery serves a selection of ciders and home made Steak & Kidney Pie amongst the food which is available at lunch time every day and on Friday and Saturday evenings.

Bridges 152–158

There are four hand-operated swing bridges between Seend and Semington's two locks. There are purpose-built steel platforms, strategically placed either side of the swing bridges for crews to jump on and off. At Semington locks there is a large covered wide dry dock with launching slipway alongside.

Tranquil Boats ▬ (01380 870654), Trailboat slipway and storage. Day boat.

The Wilts & Berks Canal Joined the Kennet & Avon between Semington Bottom Lock and the main road bridge. This once busy canal carried Somerset coal to Melksham and Swindon, with branches to Calne, Chippenham and Cricklade (where it linked up with the Thames & Severn Canal), on its way to the Thames at Abingdon. Fifty-two miles in length, it was closed in 1914, killed off by the railways. Today, the Wilts & Berks Canal Amenity Group plans to restore the waterway to navigation and welcomes new members. Information can be obtained from Chris Toms, Membership Secretary, 76 Dunnington Road, Wootton Basset, Swindon Wiltshire SN4 7EL (01628 544666) www.wilts_berks_canal.org.net

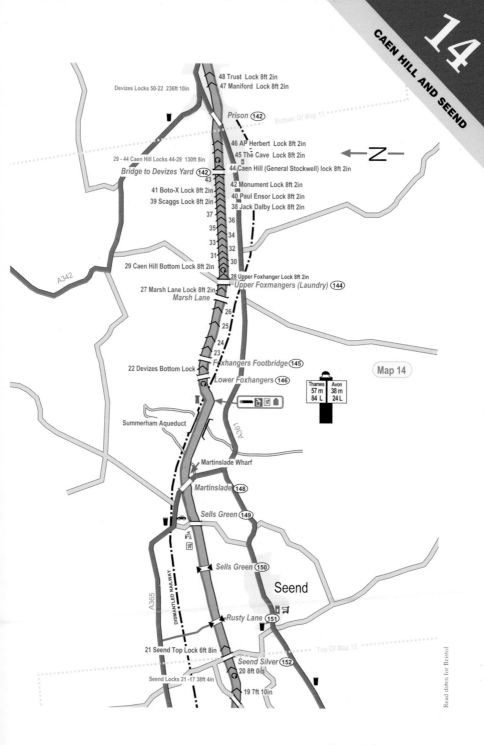

Devizes Locks 50-22 236ft 10in

48 Trust Lock 8ft 2in
47 Maniford Lock 8ft 2in

Prison (142)

Bottom Of Map 13

46 AP Herbert Lock 8ft 2in
45 The Cave Lock 8ft 2in
44 Caen Hill (General Stockwell) lock 8ft 2in

29 - 44 Caen Hill Locks 44-29 130ft 8in

Bridge to Devizes Yard (142)

43

42 Monument Lock 8ft 2in

41 Boto-X Lock 8ft 2in
39 Scaggs Lock 8ft 2in

40 Paul Ensor Lock 8ft 2in
38 Jack Dalby Lock 8ft 2in

37
36
35
34
33
32
31
30

29 Caen Hill Bottom Lock 8ft 2in

28 Upper Foxhanger Lock 8ft 2in

Upper Foxmangers (Laundry) (144)

27 Marsh Lane Lock 8ft 2in
Marsh Lane

26
25
24
23

Foxhangers Footbridge (145)

22 Devizes Bottom Lock

Lower Foxhangers (146)

Summerham Aqueduct

Martinslade Wharf

Martinslade (148)

Sells Green (149)

Sells Green (150)

Seend

Rusty Lane (151)

21 Seend Top Lock 6ft 8in

Seend Silver (152)
20 8ft 0in

Seend Locks 21 -17 38ft 4in

19 7ft 10in

Top Of Map 15

Thames	Avon
57 m	38 m
84 L	24 L

Map 14

A342

A361

A365

DISMANTLED RAILWAY

Read down for Bristol

Semington ⊟ 🛢 🅒 🍺 ⌐⊪

Little remains of the Wilts & Berks Canal junction (it provides a winding hole and pumping point for taking water back up the locks) but the toll house survives (offering bed and breakfast accommodation). Half a mile south of Bridge 160 on the busy A350 is Semington village with its Post Office and General Stores. Opposite is the Somerset Arms (Hall & Woodhouse), a 16th century coaching inn serving excellent bar and restaurant meals (booking advisable at weekend 01380 870067).

Bridge 160–166

From Semington, the canal sets off on a 5-mile pound to Bradford-on-Avon, passing over Semington Aqueduct, a sturdily built stone arch spanning a brook in typically Rennie style, before reaching Semington swing bridge (BW windlass required) and pastoral scenery beyond.

A long straight stretch follows, with a fine brick bridge at Whaddon, before reaching Hilperton Marina with its major off-channel development. The bridge at the entrance to the marina development was formerly Parson's Bridge (167), but it was taken down stone by stone, moved and rebuilt when it was replaced by a concrete bridge.

Hilperton ⊟ 🛢 🍺

The Kings Arms (Chef & Brewer) by Hilperton Bridge serves meals, and opposite is a handy petrol station, Post Office, grocer and newsagent all rolled into one and stocking firewood and coal and a cash point, at Marsh Road Stores (open 7am–10pm Mon–Sat, 8–9pm Sun).

Hilperton Marina 🔧 🛢 🍺 🅰 🛢

(01225 765243, www.moonboats.co.uk). Moorings, Pumpout, Slipway, Servicing and repairs, Boat Sales, Chandlery, and hirecraft (01787 473599).

Wessex Narrowboats ▬ 🛢 🅰 (01225 769847, www.wessexboats.co.uk). Hirecraft, Day boat hire, Pump out, Engineering, boat building and fitting out, wet dock, BSS work undertaken.

Bridges 167–171

Soon after leaving Hilperton, there are two aqueducts – Ladydown Aqueduct built to accommodate the Wiltshire, Somerset & Weymouth Railway, and Biss Aqueduct carrying the canal over the river Biss, a tributary of the Avon. John Rennie's architectural hand can be seen in the Biss aqueduct, best viewed from below after a climb down the bank.

The approach to Bradford-on-Avon is along a high embankment, with the first glimpses of the Avon valley to the north before the canal enters a cutting shielded by poplar trees. Here, after coming close together, the waterways part company to take their separate routes through the town, with the canal remaining above the valley whilst the river winds its way through the town centre.

Just before Widbrook Bridge is Bradford-on-Avon Marina, built by the Griggs family on their own farmland. Beyond Underwoods Bridge (171) on the north side are the disused workings of Bradford Clay Farm, from which puddling clay, used for lining the canal bed, was once extracted.

Bradford Marina. ▬ 🛢 🔧 🛢 🅰

(01225 864562). Moorings, Chandlery, Slipway, Boat and Engine Repairs, Craneage, Pump out, There are self catering holiday cottages on site and horse riding is available.

Sally Boats (01225 864923, www.sally-boats.ltd.uk) are based at Bradford-on-Avon Marina. Hirecraft, including short breaks and one way hires to Burghfield island with Berry Brook Boats as well as time share boats.

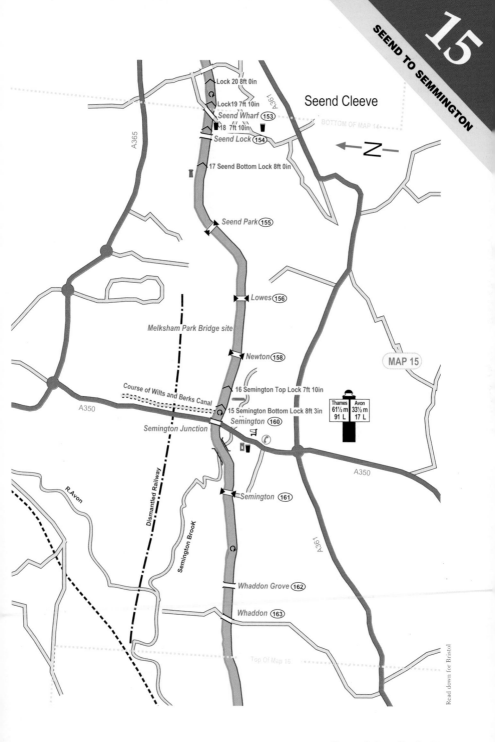

Lock 20 8ft 0in

Lock19 7ft 10in

Seend Wharf (153)

Seend Cleeve

BOTTOM OF MAP 14

18 7ft 10in

Seend Lock (154)

17 Seend Bottom Lock 8ft 0in

← N →

Seend Park (155)

Lowes (156)

MAP 15

Melksham Park Bridge site

Newton (158)

16 Semington Top Lock 7ft 10in

Course of Wilts and Berks Canal

15 Semington Bottom Lock 8ft 3in

| Thames 61½ m 91 L | Avon 33½ m 17 L |

A350

Semington (160)

Semington Junction

R.Avon

Semington (161)

A350

Semington Brook

Dismantled Railway

Whaddon Grove (162)

Whaddon (163)

Top Of Map 16

Read down for Bristol

Denise Hanlon (01225 866123) operates a boat brokerage also based at Bradford-on-Avon Marina.
The Mill House (01225 862004) at the road entrance to Bradford-on-Avon Marina is open every day for lunch and evening meals. The Beehive (Ushers) by bridge 170 offers bar and restaurant meals, open every day.

Bradford-on-Avon

All Services. EC Wed. MD Thurs. Tourist Info – 34, Silver St (01225 865797), can provide an interesting leaflet to guide your walk around the town. Bradford-on-Avon should not be missed. Not withstanding the town's links with the Iron and Saxon Ages, by far the most important (and interesting) period of its history is from the 13th to the 19th century when the wool industry dominated life and brought employment and wealth to the townsfolk. The legacy can be seen in the former merchants' houses, the stone terraces leading up from the Avon, the weavers' cottages and the riverside mills. There, too, is the little Saxon Church of St Laurence, founded in AD 705, the nine-arch 14th century Town Bridge with its Pilgrims' Chapel, The Tithe Barn (circa 1341) and Holy Trinity Church, a 12th century building with medieval wall paintings. All this can be reached from Bradford Wharf where the former gauging dock (now used as a dry dock) and original warehouse buildings have been restored and leased by the K&A Trust. The town centre, which is 10 minutes walk from the wharf is very compact and meets all shopping needs.
In the opposite, southerly, direction the main road from the bridge leads to Elms Cross Vinyard (01225 866917) which is open on Fridays, Saturdays and Mondays.

Pubs and Eating Out

The most extraordinary establishment must be Mr Salvat's 17th Century Coffee Room (01225 867474), where you can be served light meals with home baked bread and cakes by the establishment's suitably historical proprietor in appropriate surroundings. There is also a coffee house called The Scribbling Horse in Silver Street and the Bridge Tea Rooms by the bridge both provide home made fare, including lunch, 7 days a week, while The Swan Hotel in Church Street serves wholesome bar meals throughout the week (lunch and eves) and is to be recommended. There are two hostelries at the Wharf – The Barge Inn, a Free House with canalside moorings above the lock, serves full bar meals and the Canal Tavern (Wadworth), below the lock by Lower Wharf, also serves excellent bar lunch and evening meals every day. Next door is the Canalside Cafe, open Mon–Sat 9–6pm, Sun 9–7pm, where bicycles and canoes can be hired. 100 yards north of the wharf is the Curry Inn, a fully licenced Tandoori restaurant and takeaway, open every day 12–12.30pm and 5.30 to midnight, (01225 866424).
Adjacent to Bridge 171 is a Budgens supermarket, which is open every day and has a cash point, and the Beijing Paradise Chinese takeaway, open Mon–Thurs 5–11.30pm, Fri/Sat 12–2pm and 5–midnight, and Sun 5–11.30pm.

Bradford-on-Avon Wharf 〰 ⋔ ⛴
Pump out, Moorings, Slipway, Public and charter boat trips aboard the K&ACT's *Barbara McLellan* (01225 868683).

Bridge 171–Avoncliff Aqueduct Bradford Lock, with a rise and fall of 10ft 3in, was the deepest on the canal until Bath Deep Lock, at nearly 20ft, was constructed. By the lock is a K&A Trust shop and cafe (open Easter to October) and services (closed on Sundays). On the towpath immediately below the lock is the Lock Inn Cottage (01225 868068) which is

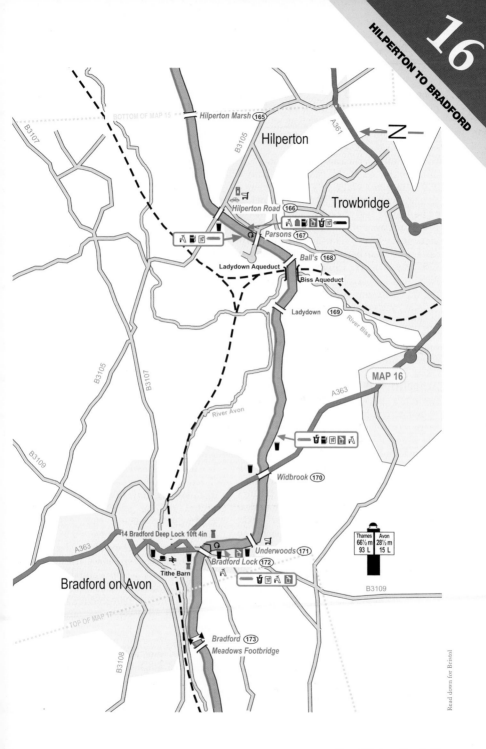

BOTTOM OF MAP 15

Hilperton Marsh 165

Hilperton

B3105

A361

N

Hilperton Road 166

Trowbridge

Parsons 167

Ladydown Aqueduct

Ball's 168

Biss Aqueduct

Ladydown 169

River Biss

B3105

B3107

MAP 16

River Avon

A363

B3109

Widbrook 170

14 Bradford Deep Lock 10ft 4in

A363

Underwoods 171

Bradford Lock 172

Tithe Barn

Bradford on Avon

	Thames	Avon
	66½ m	28½ m
	93 L	15 L

B3109

TOP OF MAP 17

Bradford 173
Meadows Footbridge

B3108

Read down for Bristol

open every day and offers canoe hire and bicycle (including tandems and trailers) hire, sales and repair as well as small day boats. Breakfast, lunch, tea and evening meals are also served.

From Bradford, the canal sets off on a ten-mile pound to Bath, passing the great Tithe Barn and entering a heavily wooded section, with the Avon in the valley below. (The canal bed from Bradford Swing Bridge to Avoncliff was re-lined with concrete in 1990). A right-angled turn (BW say sound your horn!) takes the waterway into the deep trough of Avoncliff Aqueduct and across to the other side of the valley. Restoration and relining of this Rennie masterpiece has ensured that the load has been transferred to reinforced concrete, leaving the exterior stonework untouched and the neo-classical lines in place.

Avoncliff █ ●

Avoncliff is a tiny hamlet with an unmanned railway station on the line to Bath, a restored 18th century Workhouse, and a canal bookshop offering new, sec-ondhand and antiquarian books and maps of Britain's canal heritage (open 11–4pm Easter to October); Teasels Tea Room, and The Cross Guns pub, a 16th century Free House serving food lunchtimes and evenings 7 days a week (summer week-ends get very busy so it is advisable to book (01225 862335).

Avoncliff – Bridge 175

The first two miles on the north side of the valley are known as the 'dry section', so-called after the section was drained in the early 1950s to save maintenance. The problem was an inherent one and seem-ingly incurable – porous limestone under the canal bed had defied the efforts of the navvies to seal the persistent fissures with puddle clay applied year after year, a prob-lem that was never really overcome.

In until 1976 the K&A Trust raised over £120,000 to have the entire length con-creted using labour under the Job Creation Scheme.

The scenery is breathtaking as the canal threads its way along the side of the valley under a canopy of trees with views across the Avon valley and beyond. Note the stop gates on this section to guard against pos-sible breaches and leaking aqueducts.

Limpley Stoke █ █ ◁█ The village, a five minute walk down the hill, has a Post Office stores and off licence (open Mon–Fri 8.45am–5.30pm, Sat & Sun 8.45–12 noon), The Hop Pole (Butcombe, Bass, guests) serving bar and restaurant meals in the evenings and at Sun lunch (booking recommended 01225 723134), and Nightingales Restaurant and wine bar (Tues–Sat 7pm–10.30pm, Sun 12.30–2pm), booking advisable (01225 723150).

Bridges 175–177

The canal is carried back across the river and railway on a second classical stone aqueduct, Dundas, affording further breathtaking views in both directions. There can be few monuments to the canal age more masterly than this. With massive arches striding across the valley, Doric columns, cornices and balustrades, Rennie created one of the most dramatic and audacious pieces of canal engineer-ing. There are steps down from the tow-path and it is worth climbing down to wonder at the sheer scale of the structure. It was opened in 1804 and restoration was completed in 1984. The other side is Dundas Wharf, with its original stone building, water tap and Sanitary Station, and iron crane, and the junction with the Somerset Coal Canal, which although closed in 1904, has been restored for the first quarter of a mile by the Somerset Coal Canal Co.

Picture: Scania Great Britain Ltd

A view of Dundas Aqueduct which clearly shows the fine proportions of the original structure as well as the later arch added to span the Great Western Railway. To the left the canal continues towards Bradford-on-Avon and Reading and to the bottom right it leads to Bath and Bristol. The entrance lock of the Somersetshire Coal Canal is at the top right.

The Somerset Coal Canal was surveyed by Rennie in 1793 with the aim of constructing a canal from Limpley Stoke to Paulton with a branch to Radstock. Steep gradients at Midford and Combe Hay provided continuous problems in spite of various solutions including the installation of a caisson lock, an inclined plane, and finally a flight of locks. Although the Radstock branch was never finished, the canal carried a huge tonnage of coal to places as far afield as Bristol and Reading.

Somerset Coal Canal Co

▬ 🅰 ⛟ 🗄 🗎 🗐

(The Boatyard, Brass Knocker Basin, Monkton Coombe, Bath BA2 7JD 01225 722069). Moorings, Pump Out, Solid Fuel, Engine Repairs, Chandlery,

Canalware. B&B in the lock house. The "canal company" is operated from the lock house alongside the former stop lock at the entrance to the Somerset Coal Canal by Tim Wheeldon who was responsible for restoration of the first length of the canal and construction of the moorings before the K&A was open throughout. At the end of the restored section is a canal history exhibition, café and tourist information.

Bath & Dundas Canal Co (01225 722292). Day boat, canoe and cycle hire. *Jubilee* The Kennet & Avon Canal Trust operates this 30 seat trip boat from the Somerset Coal Canal offering public and charter trips (01373 813957).

Viaduct Hotel (Ushers) serving bar food lunchtimes and eves (on the main road above).

Bridges 177–183

The stretch from Dundas Wharf to Milbrook Swing Bridge was the third section to have received the concrete bed treatment, a major task completed by BW in 1992. Thickly wooded sections and more breathtaking views down and across the valley bring the canal to Claverton, a small village on the A36 with two well known but quite different attractions – the American Museum at Claverton Manor and John Rennie's unique Claverton Pump House, sited on the Avon below the canal. The American Museum, 1.5 miles up the hill from the A36, covers 200 years of American history and art through a series of furnished rooms and exhibitions and is open from 2–5pm every day, Easter–Nov 5th, except Monday (01225 460503).

Claverton Pump House Ⓜ

Another canal-age gem – a large water-wheel operated pump which, in its day, delivered 100,000 gallons of water an hour from the river into the canal, 47ft above. Restored by the K&A Trust with help from the Bath University of Technology, the pump can be seen operating every Bank Holiday and the 4th Sunday each month between Easter and end of September (01225 483001). Today, modern electric pumps do the work and it is good to see clear river water pouring into the canal beyond the bridge.

Maintaining its level along the valley side, the canal passes more open country with fine views across to Warleigh Manor (now a College) and Bathford Church, before arriving at Bathampton Swing Bridge.

Bathampton 🍴 🏠 🍺 ⛽

A canalside village with The George Inn (Courage) serving wholesome bar meals everyday including Sundays (lunchtimes and eves), and The Bathampton Mill, a Beefeater pub and restaurant, five min-utes walk northwards towards an historic toll bridge over the Avon. The Post Office Stores in Bathampton's High Street to the south are open Mon–Sat (half day Wed) and there is a mini-market and paper shop at the top of Dark Lane beyond the bridge which is open from 5.30am every day with early closing on Sunday. St Nicholas Church is 19th century and has an Australian chapel.

Bridge 183–188

The canal heads west towards Bath past green fields and gardens to the south, while the railway keeps company on the north side in a cutting. The first glimpse of the city is across the Avon valley, where rows of Georgian houses spread out over the hillsides. Entry to the city is through Sydney Gardens, a fashionable quarter in Georgian times, whose patrons insisted that the waterway should be hidden, as far as possible, from their gaze. The result is a combination of short tunnels and elegant cast-iron bridges over a cutting, with Cleveland House, formerly the headquarters of the Kennet & Avon Canal Company, perched on top of one of the tunnels. Sydney Wharf beyond is now the base for the *John Rennie*, a restaurant boat for private charter, offering public trips.

Arrival at Bath top lock, where there are 48- hour moorings overlooked by a row of Georgian houses, sets just the right mood for the final descent, via Widcombe's six locks, down to the Avon.

Bath Narrowboats 🛥 ⛽ 🔧

(At Sydney Wharf, 01225 447276, www.bath-narrowboats.co.uk). Offer a smiley service including Pumpout. Boat fitting, painting, breakdown repairs and call out service. Also based at Sydney Wharf are the passenger trip boat *John Rennie* and timeshare boats operated by RCI Europe based in Kettering. Details are online at www.canaltime.com.

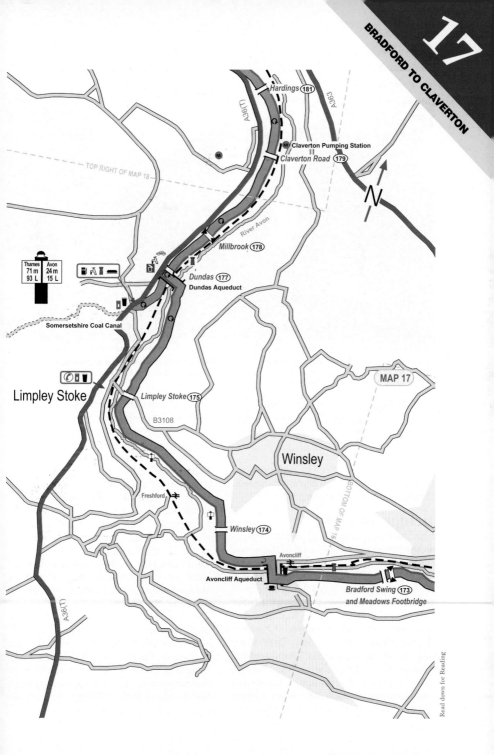

Hardings (181)

Claverton Pumping Station

Claverton Road (179)

A36(T)

A363

TOP RIGHT OF MAP 18

River Avon

Millbrook (178)

Thames	Avon
71 m	24 m
93 L	15 L

Dundas (177)
Dundas Aqueduct

Somersetshire Coal Canal

Limpley Stoke

Limpley Stoke (175)

B3108

MAP 17

Winsley

Freshford

Winsley (174)

Avoncliff

Avoncliff Aqueduct

Bradford Swing (173)
and Meadows Footbridge

BOTTOM OF MAP 16

Read down for Reading

The attractive exterior of the ingenious Claverton Pumping Station where a waterwheel driven by the river Avon in turn drives pumps to lift river Avon water to the canal, which runs at a higher level out of view to the left.

Bath Hotelboat Co (01225 448846). Full board cruises and special interest holidays aboard a professionally crewed purpose-built wide beam boat.

Bridge 188 Shops by Sydney Wharf bridge, include a Post Office, off licence, butcher, grocer and newsagent.

Bridge 188–194

The locks and their attendant iron bridges appear to be so much a part of the scene that it is as if Bath has grown up around them. There is, however one exception, the joining of locks 8 and 9 to form one of Britain's deepest canal locks, with a fall of 19ft 5in. This leads to Bath Bottom Lock, past the splendidly restored Ebenezer Baptist Chapel, the modern Bath Hotel and adjoining basin and Thimble Mill. The building and its attendant chimney stack was one of two pumping stations (all that remains of the other is an elegant chimney stack by Abbey View Lock) which

pumped water back up the flight from the Avon to augment Claverton's supplies to the nine mile pound.

There are two public moorings on the river in Bath – the picturesque one below Pulteney Weir about half a mile up-stream from the junction with the Avon where a fee is charged, while the second is below Churchill Bridge (No 198). Both are centrally placed and it is advisable to use chains to secure your craft to ward off would-be night time pranksters.

Don't forget to make allowance for the current immediately at the tail of Widcombe Bottom Lock as you enter, or leave, the river.

Those intent of navigating above Poultney weir may do so on trip boats (01225 428422 or 01225 466407) which operate (between Easter and October) from moorings immediately above the weir to Bathampton or in a rowing boat or punt hired from Bath Boating Station in Forrester Road (01225 466407).

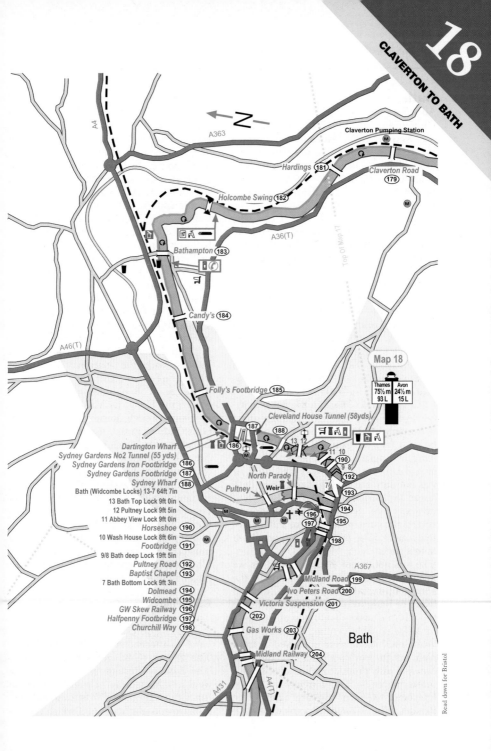

Claverton Pumping Station

Hardings (181)

Claverton Road (179)

Holcombe Swing (182)

A363

A4

A36(T)

Bathampton (183)

Candy's (184)

A46(T)

Folly's Footbridge (185)

Map 18

	Thames	Avon
	75½ m	24½ m
	93 L	15 L

Cleveland House Tunnel (58yds)

(187) (188)

Dartington Wharf
Sydney Gardens No2 Tunnel (55 yds) (186)
Sydney Gardens Iron Footbridge (186)
Sydney Gardens Footbridge (187)
Sydney Wharf (188)
Bath (Widcombe Locks) 13-7 64ft 7in
13 Bath Top Lock 9ft 0in
12 Pultney Lock 9ft 5in
11 Abbey View Lock 9ft 0in
Horseshoe (190)
10 Wash House Lock 8ft 6in
Footbridge (191)
9/8 Bath deep Lock 19ft 5in
Pultney Road (192)
Baptist Chapel (193)
7 Bath Bottom Lock 9ft 3in
Dolmead (194)
Widcombe (195)
GW Skew Railway (196)
Halfpenny Footbridge (197)
Churchill Way (198)

13 12

11 10
(190)
9 8
(192)

North Parade

Pultney

Weir

7
(193)

(194)

(195)

(196)
(197)

(198)

Midland Road (199)
Ivo Peters Road (200)
Victoria Suspension (201)

A367

(202)

Gas Works (203)

Bath

Midland Railway (204)

A431

A4(T)

Bath

All Services. Tourist Info, Abbey Churchyard (01225 477101). Launderette – Claverton Street, Widcombe. Bath owes its origins to the hot springs beneath the city which have been producing water at a constant temperature of 46.5°C for close-on 8000 years. It was Bladud, father of King Lear who first discovered the springs in 500 BC. To the Celts, the springs were sacred to their deity Sulis, to whom they gave offerings. But it was the Romans, soon after they landed in Britain in AD 43, who developed the waters for bathing and medicinal purposes and later, as a focal point for social gatherings. They linked Sulis with Minerva, a Roman Goddess of health and healing, and built a temple in their joint honour, parts of which along with a reconstruction of the entire Roman Bath complex can be seen today. The Roman name for Bath was Aquae Sulis (The Waters of Sulis).

Little is known of Bath in the Saxon period apart from the foundation of a monastery in AD 675 which later became famous for the Coronation of Edgar as King of England in the presence of the archbishops of Canterbury and York. It was not until the Middle Ages, when Bath began to flourish again on the strength of its wool trade, that it attracted hopefuls in search of a cure from its warm and medicinal waters. The present Abbey was built at this time.

The splendours of Bath however, as we know them, did not materialise until the 18th century, when Beau Nash, dubbed 'King of Bath,' was appointed to clean up the city and make it into one of Europe's most fashionable centres. Architect John Wood and his son were employed as town planners to provide elegant accommodation and duly produced some of the city's masterpieces – The Circus, the Royal Crescent, Queen Square and The Parades. The Assembly Rooms were built to cater for the increasing numbers of aristocratic visitors, and an elegant Pump Room where they could gather to take the waters. Pulteney Bridge, with its attendant shops, is the work of Robert Adam.

The opportunity to view this magnificent Georgian city should not be missed. Open top bus tours run frequently from Grand Parade and the Abbey, whilst free, guided walking tours can be joined outside the Pump Room. The main attractions are all within walking distance of the centre and include; the Roman Baths Museum and Pump Room in Abbey Churchyard (9am to 5pm daily, 01225 477785), the Abbey, the Assembly Rooms and Museum of Costume in Bennett Street; No 1, Royal Crescent (a restored Georgian residence); Mr Bowler's Soda Water factory, recreated in Bath Industrial Heritage Centre on Julian Road; the National Centre of Photography in Milsom Street; the Museum of Bookbinding in Manvers Street; the Holburne Museum (paintings by Gainsborough, Reynolds and Stubbs), Great Pultney Street; the Postal Museum, Broad Street; Museum of English Naive Art, The Paragon; Sally Lunn's Kitchen Museum (and Refreshment House), North Parade Passage; The Guildhall, entrance via the Market and The William Herschel Museum in a restored town house of 1764 at 19 New King Street, housing displays of Herschel's work as a musician and astronomer (he discovered Uranus), the garden has also been returned to its Georgian condition.

Eating out

There are dozens of places in Bath catering for all tastes, from morning coffee, lunch or afternoon tea at the Pump Room, The Boater (Courage) serving lunches, The Bathtub Restaurant (open 7 days a week), Maxson's Diner, (serving American 'Cajun' food 7 days a week), No. 5 Bistro and Marmaris (a Turkish restau-

Cleveland House, once headquarters of the Kennet & Avon Canal Co stands impressively atop its tunnel.

rant open 7 days a week) in Grand Parade. In Widcombe, by Bath Deep Lock, is The Ram (Courage) and The White Hart (Whitbread) serving bar meals lunch times only, and The Ring of Bells (Free House) serving bar snacks. Pubs serving real ale and food are in abundance too.

Shopping

The main shopping thoroughfare is formed by Milsom Street, Union Street, Stall Street and Southgate, on which many of the banks, big-name shops, supermarkets and boutiques are to be found. Northumberland Place and The Corridor are passageways lined with small shops and places to eat, while The Podium and Shire's Yard are two shopping precincts. The full range of basic foods is also available throughout the week in The Guildhall Market. Down the Avon Sainsbury's supermarket, which incorporates parts of the Somerset & Dorset Joint Railway's former Green Park Station, is easily reached from bridge 199.

Bridge 195–206 As you set off downstream from Widcombe pause a moment and wonder at the flood marks cut into the wall above the towpath under bridge 195 – that of 15th November 1894 is at least 10ft above the present towpath! The most notable features heading west out of Bath on the Avon are the bridges, beginning with Widcombe Bridge (195), leading to the railway station, then the great Western's Skew Railway Bridge (196) followed by the Half Penny Footbridge (197), which carries the towpath (also known as the Avon Walkway) across to the north side and down to Broad Quay and the public moorings beyond Churchill Way Bridge (198). Between bridges 197 and 198, aligning with the railway's girder bridge, now in the midst of the main road roundabout, was 'Old Bridge'. Built in 1798, this included remains of St Lawrence Bridge which dated from 1340. There is little evidence of the once busy quayside at Broad Quay, where barges and narrowboats collected and discharged their cargoes.

After Midland Road Bridge is the former Somerset & Dorset Joint Railway Bridge, now carrying traffic on Ivo Peters Road to Sainsbury's supermarket, in the former Green Park Station, followed by the Victoria Suspension Bridge, built in 1836 and utilising uniquely slanted suspension rods. Next is Midland Road Bridge and another disused railway bridge which now carries the Bristol–Bath Cycle Path, much used by commuting and leisure cyclists.

Beyond, the river divides, taking the navigation into a canal cut to the right and Weston Lock where there is a water point. At Dolphin Bridge is the Dolphin Inn, which serves Wadworths, Marstons and Flowers real ales and bar meals every day with OAP specials on Thursdays – moor either side of bridge.

Bridge 208 ⛽ ⛽ 🍴 A short distance from Newbridge on the nearby A4 road is a Park & Ride service into the city centre and beyond is a Post Office stores. Beyond the bridge is The Boathouse riverside bar & restaurant (01225 482584) with temporary moorings. The Edwardian-styled Pavilion with its choice of bars and excellent food (including cream teas) is well worth a visit – it is advisable to book for Sat and Sun meals.

Bath Marina (01225 424301). Permanent moorings and a large caravan park but access is difficult for casual visitors.

Bridge 208–210

At Newbridge, the towpath crosses from the north to the south side. The river meanwhile, finally leaves the environs of Bath, heads west into open country and into a series of bends before Kelston Park appears on the north bank, with wooded hillsides beyond. A long, wide straight flanked by the main railway line to the west, leads to Kelston Lock on the right hand side as the river divides.

Saltford Marina ⛽ 🅿 🏕 (01225 872226) All services. Pump-out, Permanent moorings, Brokerage. The Riverside restaurant & bar is part of the marina complex and serves morning coffee, lunches, afternoon teas and evening meals as well as bar food, 7 days a week.

Saltford 🍴 🅿 🍴 Access to Saltford is best from the marina. There is a Co-op, off-licence, newsagent, Post Office stores and Indian and Chinese takeaways astride the A4 road. The Crown serves food all day and the Bird-in-Hand (Courage, Archers and Ciders) in the older part of the village (half-a-mile down the road which follows the river), serves bar meals 7-days a week. St Mary's Church, dates back to Norman times, and Saltford Manor is reputed to be one of the oldest inhabited houses in England.

Bridge 210–211

Below Kelston Lock are Mill Island Moorings, the mill being a former brass mill which ceased rolling brass in the 1920s. A mile on from Kelston Lock is Saltford Sailing Club, Sheppards Boat Yard (boat builders) and Saltford Lock on the left hand side. The Jolly Sailor (Courage) serves lunches and evening meals everyday; booking is advisable for the restaurant (01225 873002). Mooring is very restricted here. Saltford Pottery, behind the Jolly Sailor, specialises in animal figures and is open weekdays only. Kelston Brass Mill on the north side beyond the weir has been renovated and the adjacent row of cottages are believed to be some of the oldest surviving workers cottages. The river now turns west, parallel to the A431 to Swineford.

Bristol Boats (01225 872032). At Sheppard's Boatyard. Chandlery, Boat Sales, Outboard Repairs, Slipway, (limited 20ft mooring).

Dutch-built luxemotor barge *Clementina* occasionally visits the Bristol Avon from her base on the Warwickshire Avon. She is seen here winding below Pultney Weir in Bath with the famous Pultney Bridge occupying the background.

Swineford ⚏ ▯ ▮ Ⓒ So-called after pigs made the first crossing of the river at the time of Bladud (the same fellow who discovered the hot springs in Bath around 500 BC). There is a water point and sanitary station on the south bank, just before the village. A footpath leads up to the village from the north bank of the river below the lock. The Swan (Courage) serves home cooked bar meals and snacks at lunchtime and restaurant meals in evenings (but not on Sunday evenings). Booking is advised at weekends (0117 932 3101).

Bridge 211–214

From Swineford Lock, the river passes through low lying, open pastureland and under another disused Midland Railway bridge carrying the Bristol–Bath Cycle Path. The river Boyd joins here as the Avon continues to wind its leisurely way towards Keynsham. On the approach to the town at former commercial wharfs is Phoenix Marine immediately downstream of which the river forms a giant horse shoe bend. At Keynsham, the lock is on the right-hand side where the river enters a narrow cutting. By White Hart Bridge is The Lock Keeper (Free House with Youngs, Smiles and guests) serving bar and restaurant meals 7 days a week, eve restaurant bookings advisable (0117 986 2383). The Brassmill, just over the river from the lock cut, serves Brewers' Fayre meals lunch and evening, seven days a week as well as Wadworths and guest beers.

Phoenix Marine ⚓ ⚒ ▮ ▤ ▮ (0117 986 4181) Pump Out, Craneage, Boats built and fitted out.

Avon Canal Boat Centre. (0117-986 1168) Repairs, Chandlery, Pump-out, Boat Sales.

Portavon Marina. (0117 986 1626) All services, Chandlery. Restricted to craft of 30ft maximum.

Keynsham

All services. From County Bridge (214), the town is at the top of the hill (about half-a-mile walk) where all shopping needs may be met. There is a choice of pubs all offering bar meals – The Ship Inn with a choice of real ales and shove ha'penny, The Pioneer (Free House), The Trout Tavern (Courage), and The London Inn (Halls). Of note is the large church dating back to the 13th century.

A walk in the opposite, northerly, direction along the A4174 leads to Bitton and the Avon Valley Railway (Talking Timetable 0117 932 7296, www.avonvalleyrailway.co.uk) where the station is open (free admission) every day in summer with steam trains at weekends (plus Wednesdays in August).

Bridge 214–Hanham Lock

On leaving Keynsham Lock, the valley narrows and is overlooked on the south side by a red brick factory (circa 1923) at Somerdale, former home of Fry's Chocolate but now owned by Cadbury Schweppes. Remnants of the terminus of the Avon & Gloucestershire Railway, a horse-drawn tramway, can be seen opposite the Cadbury's factory – coal was transported from Coalpit Heath to the wharf and despatched by river.

Continuing on its circuitous route, the river passes Cleeve Wood on the north bank before turning sharply to the north at Park Corner, where southern hills begin to encroach on the river leading to Hanham Mills and Hanham Lock. Again the river divides, with the lock cutting to the left. On the right is a small hamlet with two pubs – The Chequers Inn (Free House) (0117 967 4242), serving bar and restaurant meals throughout the week, with booking advisable for the Sunday lunchtime carvery, and offering overnight moorings. Next door is The Old Lock & Weir (Free House, with Theakston's, Marston's and guest beers) which serves food·at lunch time and evenings every day except Sunday evenings. A friendly and traditional local – somewhat below flood level!

Hanham Lock

Hanham Lock is No 1 on the Kennet & Avon Navigation and the limit of British Waterways jurisdiction; it is also the tidal limit of the Avon. Licences may be purchased from the toll office by the lock for passage into Bristol Docks (see under Bristol City Docks on pages 4 and 14) and the lock keeper is pleased to offer advice on the passage to Bristol and tide times.

Hanham–Netham Lock

It is normally possible to navigate from Hanham straight through Netham Lock (where the gates are left open) and into the Feeder Canal to the Floating Harbour, a distance of 7 miles (11.2 kilometres) in daylight hours. However, at high Spring Tides when Netham lock gates are closed, extreme care should be taken when navigating this section. Details and a table showing times of these "Stopgate Tides" are available from the Bristol Harbour Master (see under Bristol City Docks, page 14).

The tidal river enters a steeply wooded valley with Fox's Wood to the south and Hencliff Wood to the north. What little remains of Hanham Colliery Wharf can be seen on the bend before Conham Vale while on the south bank below Broom Hill is Beese's Tea Gardens (circa 1846) which offers the only sustenance and water point between Hanham and Bristol.

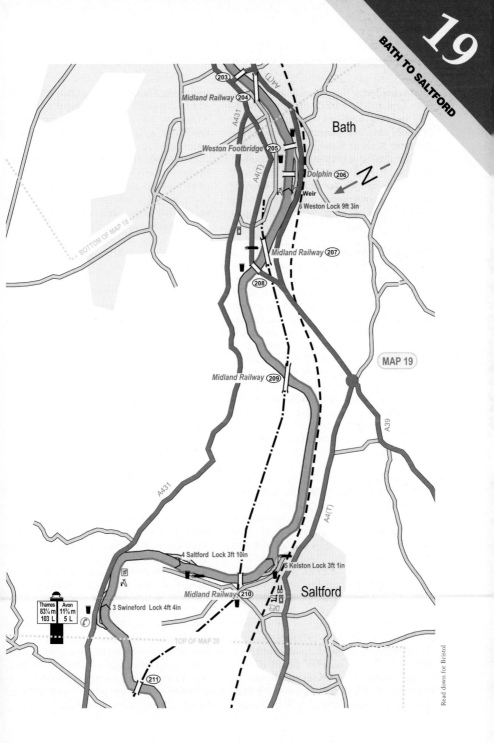

203

Midland Railway 204

Weston Footbridge 205

Bath

Dolphin 206

Weir

6 Weston Lock 9ft 3in

Midland Railway 207

208

MAP 19

Midland Railway 209

A39

A431

A4(T)

4 Saltford Lock 3ft 10in

5 Kelston Lock 3ft 1in

Midland Railway 210

Saltford

Thames	Avon
83¼ m	11¾ m
103 L	5 L

3 Swineford Lock 4ft 4in

TOP OF MAP 20

211

BOTTOM OF MAP 18

After completing the horse-shoe bend, the river says goodbye to its rural surroundings and enters Bristol's suburbs, passing St James Park to the south. On the apex of the next bend is Crew's Hole, a former industrial complex where coal was mined and tar manufactured. Netham Lock (where the keeper monitors VHF channel 73) appears abruptly on the right after passing large wharves now redeveloped with new housing.

Netham–Junction Lock

For the next mile, the navigation is known as The Feeder Canal, an artificial waterway bypassing a meandering stretch of the river to the south. Sanctioned as part of the Bristol Dock Act of 1803, the Feeder was cut to aid navigation and to supply Bristol's Floating Harbour with water. There is little to commend it scenically as it passes through a heavily industrialised part of the city. At Totterdown, at the end of the Feeder Canal straight, is the point at which the New Cut (to the south) rejoined the natural course of the river via a lock which has long since disappeared.

The next bridge carries the main line into Temple Meads Station and the original terminus of Brunel's Great Western Railway – keep to the right of the two arches. From here, it is important to know bridge opening times and navigational instructions as laid down by the City Council and published in the Information for Boat Owners and Visitors Guide (see under Bristol City Docks on page 14). After St Philip's Bridge, craft should sound their horns before passing the next three bridges. (Redcliffe Bascule and Princes Street Swing bridges are manned during the daytime and craft must observe the semaphore or light signals and may contact the keeper on VHF channel 73).

To the south beyond Redcliffe Bridge is Bathurst Basin, another, now closed, access from the river and now the moorings of the Cabot Cruising Club (0117 926 8318), complete with lightship club house. There are two official mooring places in the Floating Harbour, complete with fresh water and 230 volt power points; both are just beyond the Princes Street Swing Bridge – Narrow Quay in St Augustine's Reach on the right (note that the top of the quay wall is 10ft from water level), and on the left at Prince's Wharf. There are other mooring spots for visiting boats – at Bathurst Quay, Welsh Back and in front of the Lloyds Building, but with limited facilities.

The Floating Harbour

Speed limit – 6 mph. This 2.5 mile expanse of water in the heart of the city is Bristol's focal point for recreation and leisure, bringing together its historic maritime past and creating a waterside amenity rich in variety. Its origins lie in the early 19th century, when, as one of the major ports serving the Americas, Bristol began to suffer with increasing competition from Liverpool and other seaward ports. Constructed to the designs of William Jessop, the Floating Harbour was built as a massive deep water dock along the original course of the Avon, necessitating a diversion of the river to the south in a channel called the New Cut. Opened in 1809, the Floating Harbour did little to improve trade as the new harbour dues, imposed by the private dock company to pay for the work, were too high.

Bristol's prosperity had been built on the import of tobacco, sugar, chocolate and sherry as well as on slave trading and ship building (hence the origin of the term 'ship shape and Bristol fashion'). Today, the quayside buildings have been turned into shops, restaurants, museums, arts centres and exhibition areas while the harbour provides for a number of waterborne activities including power boat racing, regattas, boat rallies, sailing and fishing.

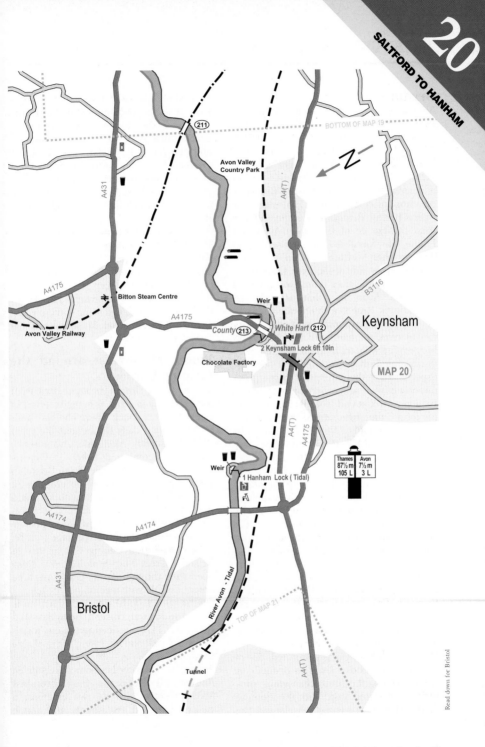

211

Avon Valley
Country Park

A431

A4175

Bitton Steam Centre

Avon Valley Railway

A4175

Weir

County 213

White Hart 212

2 Keynsham Lock 6ft 10in

Chocolate Factory

Keynsham

B3116

MAP 20

A4(T)

A4175

Thames	Avon
87½ m	7½ m
105 L	3 L

Weir

1 Hanham Lock (Tidal)

A4174

A4174

A431

Bristol

River Avon - Tidal

TOP OF MAP 21

A4(T)

Tunnel

BOTTOM OF MAP 19

Read down for Bristol

Bristol

All Services. Zoo. MD Mon–Fri. Tourist Info, Harbourside, behind the amphitheatre (0117 926 0767, http://tourism.bristol.gov.uk). Launderettes: 78 Alma Road and 34 Princess Victoria Street. The name Bristol is derived from the Saxon word Bregstow meaning 'place of bridge'. That place was where Bristol Bridge now stands, at the then confluence of the rivers Avon and Frome, which enabled the early settlers to develop their settlements on the high ground either side of the river. During the 13th century the river Frome was diverted into the Avon at what is now St Augustine's Reach, a deliberate move to develop Bristol as a major port ahead of its nearby rival, the hamlet of Redcliffe. The burgeoning wool trade in the west country during the 15th century led to a boost in exports from the port with consequent imports of wine and other commodities.

Explorers too, set off from Bristol, including John Cabot, who returned with tales of discovery notably 'New-found-land'. In the 17th century ships from the city became heavily involved in the slave trade, shipping Africans to the West Indies and returning to the city laden with cargoes of sugar, rum and tobacco. However, the war with America in the 1770s and the abolition of the slave trade in 1833 struck a devastating blow to Bristol's fortunes from which the port never really recovered. The increase in tolls to pay for the new Floating Harbour drove many ships away, including Brunel's *Great Western*, built in Bristol to link his railway with New York; such was the high level of Bristol's harbour dues that the ship was forced to move its operations to Liverpool.

However, ship-building continued, diversifying from wooden ships to Brunel's ss *Great Britain*, the first ocean-going propeller-driven iron ship. With the increase in the size of sea-going vessels and the somewhat unpredictable and hazardous river passage, trade diminished still further until the decision was reached to develop new port facilities at Avonmouth and Portishead. Today, the Floating Harbour has bounced back from its years of decline and is now basking in its past glories, as reflected in the museums and exhibitions which have sprung up around its quaysides.

The Tourist Information Centre can provide a Bristol Heritage Walk leaflet which will guide the explorer to many of these sights in a leisurely two to three hour stroll. One of the, very few, disappointments is the overpowering 'The Point' development overshadowing and crowding against the Industrial Museum and the quays at Wapping Wharf.

Places of interest around the Floating Harbour

The ss *Great Britain*, brought back from the Falklands in 1970, is being restored in Great Western Dock where she was built in 1843 (open daily throughout the year) (0117 926 0680). Alongside, and accessible with a combined ticket, is Cabot's *Matthew* in which he sailed from Bristol in 1497. This replica made the crossing in 1997 and if nothing else visitors should marvel at the contrast in size and technology between the two ships. Next door is the associated Maritime Heritage Centre, a free exhibition tracing the history of Bristol's great ship-building era, (also open daily throughout the year). All three are accessible with a combined ticket

On the same (south) side of the harbour is Bristol Industrial Museum open Sat–Wed (0117 925 1470), reflecting the city's rich industrial past and operating the dockside railway.

Across the Floating Harbour alongside St Augustine's Reach is the Watershed Media Centre with its two cinemas, a gallery, bar and restaurant, and much

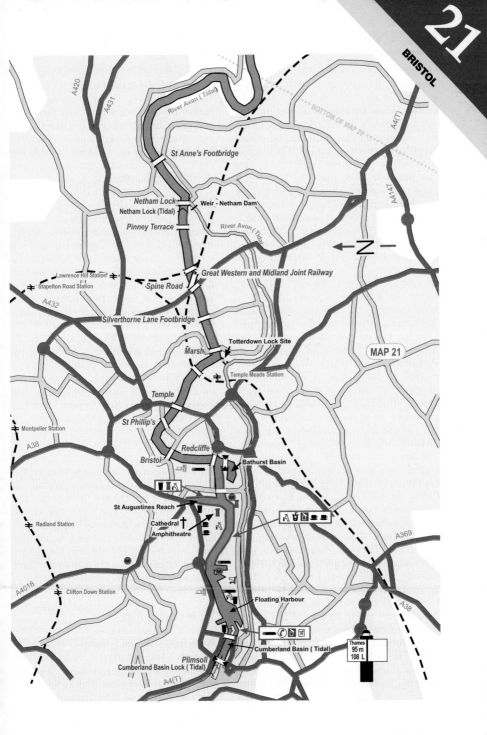

River Avon (Tidal)

St Anne's Footbridge

Netham Lock
Netham Lock (Tidal) Weir - Netham Dam

Pinney Terrace

River Avon (Tidal)

←N—

A420
A431

A4(T)

A4147

BOTTOM OF MAP 20

Lawrence Hill Station
Stapelton Road Station

Great Western and Midland Joint Railway

Spine Road

A432

Silverthorne Lane Footbridge

Totterdown Lock Site

Marsh

Temple Meads Station

MAP 21

Temple

St Phillip's

Montpelier Station
A38

Redcliffe

Bristol

Bathurst Basin

St Augustines Reach

Cathedral
Amphitheatre

Redland Station

Floating Harbour

A369

Clifton Down Station

A4018

M

M

A38

Cumberland Basin (Tidal)

Plimsoll
Cumberland Basin Lock (Tidal)

A4(T)

Thames
95 m
108 L

more all by the water front ready to explore. St Augustine's Reach, the short section of the harbour extending into the city northwards, is the last vestige of the river Frome and has, at its top end, a statue of Neptune dating back to 1723.

West of St Augustine's reach extensive changes have taken place in the last few years with construction of extensive office development, the Tourist Information Centre, and the @Bristol complex including an Imax Cinema, and 'Wildscreen' Cinema which specialises in ecology and nature and a number of restaurants and café's.

In College Green is Bristol Cathedral, (open daily 8am–6pm), established in 1140 and once the monastic Abbey of St Augustine, which contains a Norman Chapter House and 12th century Lady Chapel. Cabot Tower, Brandon Hill off Park Street (open dawn to dusk), was built in 1897 to commemorate the 4th centenary of John Cabot's voyage of discovery to North America from Bristol – fabulous city views from top of 105ft tower. The City Museum & Art Gallery, Queen's Road, (open daily 10–5pm) house outstanding collections of European ceramics and glass, a noteworthy Natural History Gallery and Egyptology Gallery. The Exchange and The Nails is in Corn Street – in front of the building on the pavement are four nails used for cash transactions in former times – hence the expression 'pay on the nail'. Harvey's Wine Museum, is in Denmark Street, (open Mon–Fri, 10-5pm, closed lunchtimes; Sat & Sun 2–5pm)(there is also an excellent restaurant). St Mary's Redcliffe, Redcliffe Way (open every day), classic 15th century Perpendicular architecture and a favourite of Elizabeth I. John Wesley's Chapel, the oldest Methodist Chapel in the world is at 36 The Horsefair and open from 10–4pm Monday to Saturday. Brunel's Clifton Suspension Bridge (702ft) spans the Avon Gorge in spectacular fashion. Opened in 1864, it is still in daily use as a road bridge. It now has a visitor centre near the north end open April to September 10am to 6pm Mon–Sat with reduced hours on Sundays and from October to March (0117 974 4664). Bristol Zoo, also in Clifton, is open daily throughout the year.

Eating Out

Bristol offers international cuisine through dozens of eating places – details may be had from the Tourist Information Centre. On the waterfront is Brunel's Buttery (Wapping Wharf) specialising in home-made pies, cakes and sandwiches, open 7-days a week; the Quayside Cafe serving hot meals and snacks from 10.30 – 10.30pm every day at Narrow Quay. There are bars and restaurants either side of St Augustine's Reach in the Arnolfini Centre (former tea warehouses of the 1830s) and in the Watershed Centre. At Welsh Back on the water (by Bristol Bridge) is the Glass Boat Restaurant, open Mon–Fri, breakfast, lunch and dinner, Sat dinner. In King Street are the Llandoger Trow, open every day; King William's Ale House offering pub meals; open every day; the Royal Navy Volunteer also serving hot meals; the Cathay Rendezvous Chinese restaurant and Renato's Taverna and Artista pizza bar and restaurant. On the north side of the Floating Harbour almost opposite ss *Great Britain* is The Shoots Floating Bar and Restaurant (0117 925 0597), a former Severn barge which is open at lunch times Tuesday to Friday and evenings Monday to Saturday.

Waterside pubs

The Cottage, Baltic Wharf; The Waterfront Tavern, Narrow Quay; the Ostrich Inn, Bathurst Basin; The Lightship, a floating pub moored alongside Welsh Back; the Nova Scotia in Hotwell Road, and The Pump House in

A hotel boat explores Bristol's Floating Harbour, Brunel's *Great Britain* occupies the Great Western Drydock beyond and the full size replica of Cabot's *Mathew* appears miniature by comparison, to the left.

Merchants Road, Hotwells, overlooking the harbour. The Shakespeare Tavern, 68 Princes Street, near the Arnolfini and The Bridge Inn, 16 Passage Street, near the former brewery said to be Bristol's smallest pub are also worth investigation.

There is a useful, and handy, general store in Mardyke Road by the 'New Cut' of the tidal river Avon close to the marina.

Boat Yard facilities

Bristol Marina ⛽ 🗑 ⛺ 🛢 (0117 921 3198) (Hanover Place on the south side of the Floating Harbour) All services, Pump out, Moorings, Craneage and straddle lift, Slipway, Launderette, Engine and boat repairs, building and sales. Chandlery is provided by adjacent **Force 4 Chandlery** (0117 926 8396) which has an extensive stock to suit both deep sea and inland craft.

Anglo Welsh Waterway Holidays ⛽ 🛢 🛢 (0117 927 7107, www.anglowelsh-group.plc.uk) Avon Quay, Cumberland Basin, close to Junction Lock. Hire craft and day boat, Pump Out, Repairs.

Boat trips

Bristol Boat Company (0117 927 3416). Daily in summer, weekend only in winter scheduled ferry services around the docks between numerous well signed landing places, one-hour tours and meals afloat trips.

The Bristol Packet Wapping Wharf, Gas Ferry Road (0117 926 8157 & 973 5315). Boat trips in narrowboat Redshank and mv Tower Belle. One-hour City Docks Tour, trips to the Avon Gorge, Beese's Tea Gardens at Conham, the Chequers at Hanham or even Bath (Easter to Sept).

Bristol & Bath Cruises (0117 821 4307). Private party, candlelight and Sunday lunch cruises.

Passage down the tidal Avon from Cumberland Basin is not recommended for canal craft – see page 5.